Rhythms
of Rest

Rhythms of Rest

40 DEVOTIONS for WOMEN ON THE MOVE

SUZAN D. JOHNSON COOK
and Contributors

Our Daily Bread
Publishing™

Rhythms of Rest: 40 Devotions for Women on the Move
© 2021 by Suzan D. Johnson Cook

Requests for permission to quote from this book should be directed to: Permissions Department, Our Daily Bread Publishing, PO Box 3566, Grand Rapids, MI 49501, or contact us by email at permissionsdept@odb.org.

"Metamorphic." © Copyright B. Williams Waters. Used by permission. All rights reserved.

"His Perfect Plans," and "The Damascus Road" adapted from *By Faith: Adventures and Reflections on Walking with God Here and Abroad* by Nancy Gavilanes. Used by permission.

Bible permissions can be found on page 223

Interior design by Kris Nelson/StoryLook Design

Library of Congress Cataloging-in-Publication Data

Names: Johnson Cook, Suzan D. (Suzan Denise), 1957- author.
Title: Rhythms of rest : 40 devotions for women on the move / Suzan Johnson Cook and contributors.
Description: Grand Rapids, MI : Our Daily Bread Publishing, [2021] | Summary: "Rhythms of Rest provides a respite for you to simply be still and spend time with the Lord. These 40 meaningful devotions from leaders in Black and multicultural communities and churches invite you to pause and reflect on Scripture as you ponder topics like soul care, sisterhood, seasons of life, and Spirit-led living"-- Provided by publisher.
Identifiers: LCCN 2021016629 | ISBN 9781640700758 (paperback)
Subjects: LCSH: Christian women--Religious life. | Minority women--Religious life. | Devotional literature. | BISAC: RELIGION / Christian Living / Devotional
Classification: LCC BV4527 .J645 2021 | DDC 242/.643--dc23
LC record available at https://lccn.loc.gov/2021016629

Printed in the United States of America

21 22 23 24 25 26 27 28 / 8 7 6 5 4 3 2 1

To God be the glory
for the great things God has done!

To my parents,
the late Dorothy C. and Wilbert T. Johnson

• ——— *CONTENTS* ——— •

But You, Lord,

are a shield around me,

My glory,

and the One who lifts my head.

I was crying out to the Lord

with my voice,

And He answered me

from His holy mountain.

Selah

PSALM 3:3–4 (NASB)

*M*y parents, Dorothy C. and Wilbert T. Johnson, were a courageous, Christ-led and -fed couple who had the unmitigated gall to believe that working in the fields nonstop was not their destiny and would not be the end of their story.

Their love for the Lord, family, and one another, along with their work and play ethics, instilled in me from a very early age lessons on life balance—how to have fun, work hard, and play hard; how to create and become a family and an extended family of loved ones; how to bless others; and how to be authentically who I am. They knew they had a leader on their hands very early and, instead of clipping my wings, they let me fly high. They named me *Suzan*, encouraging me to *soar*, and they put in the *Z*, so that you'd remember me! They taught me the value of recreating—and taking vacations—sometimes with family and, at other times, when *I* simply need to pray, play, or *get away*.

They taught me to be well-treated by others, and to treat myself and others well, even with meager funds, and how to be respected, and to be respectful of others. How to be well rested, because they knew I'd be tested—by life, by a world that didn't always have a place for a Black girl like me, who, instead of respect, the world would often reject. They led me first, to "be saved," to be Christian. And then they wanted me to be savvy, soulfully sophisticated, stylish, brilliant, and resilient, and unapologetically Black, feminine, and human. Thanks, Mom and Dad!

Thank you to all the women in my life who have loved and cared for me: my grandmother, Leona Fisher Starnes Thomas; and my favorite aunts, Martha Springs Porcher and Katherine Hayes Cyrus, Aunt Bertha; and my forever "big sister" Katie Cannon. Thanks to my prayer partner and traveling companion, Mercedes, who knows my rhythm, oh so well, and helps me, runs interference when necessary, and holds my hand when we're passing over turbulent air pockets and through turbulent waters, literally and figuratively. And how wonderful it is to have such great adult cousins; Christian friends; extended family, Jennifer and Stephen, who share both heart and home with me; and the "waterside crew," who look in on me, and share laughter, love, and prayers.

And thanks to the countless women who have placed their trust in God, and who have not only come to all of our gatherings, conferences, and Selah by the Sea retreats, but have invested time, talent, and resources in our relationship—some of you many times over. Thank you, "WOW Women," for showing up and for sharing your fullness and your brokenness in all the sacred *sister spaces* God creates. Also to the women of faith who are on the move and who have joined the newly launched Global Black Women's Chamber of Commerce. While you are busy managing and becoming today's movers and shakers, may you find a wealth of words on wellness and wholeness, moments of pause as you learn to pivot, and may you insert times of rest and renewal as you take care of the "rest" of our communities.

Though I minister so often with women, I cannot pen this book without thanking my "guys," Chris and Sam, whom I love, and who help keep me *in step*—in rhythm and in tune with the times.

Finally, thank you to my Our Daily Bread family, especially the executive editor of Our Daily Bread Ministries Voices Collection, the Honorable Joyce Dinkins—not honorable because she's an elected official or dignitary, but because she is such a mighty woman of valor and honor. She walks in grace and with dignity, and is, like David, a person *after God's own heart*. Joyce, your writing genius and your generosity of time and of spirit are greatly appreciated. Your anointing, your excellence in execution, and your willingness to share your time, talent, and resources are immeasurable. You are an executive editor par excellence, an encourager, an equipper, a pray-er, and a sister beloved. Thank you for not only bringing the voices of our sisters together in this volume, but for also *being* one of us, one with us. You've come not to sit and watch us, but to participate with us, and be among us as a godly, female presence with Jesus's Spirit.

He leads me beside

the still waters.

He restores my soul.

PSALM 23:2–3 (NKJV)

Welcome to Selah

Sisters who care for others, sisters who work full time, part time, at home, sisters who are looking for balance and peace. This is the place for you, where we celebrate God, and more importantly, learn to rest in God. These devotions are designed for women of God who trust in God and want to continue to find rest in God's presence.

You're invited to a *God party* through these devotions. One that has no boundaries, requires no walls between us, but that unites and connects us across generations, cultures, differences, and distances.

Thank you for your open hearts. May you be blessed; become excited; be empowered, enlightened, engaged, and encouraged by these devotions, as we focus on ways we can rest in God. We pray you will be moved by our diverse voices and the range of our experiences, and touched by God's almighty presence and power as you enter, read, reflect—as we *selah*.

Selah is the word that appears in the book of Psalms seventy-one times, and is often repeated within a single psalm. *Selah* occurs three times in the book of Habakkuk. Although debated, the wider use and meaning of this Hebrew word is "to pause . . . to reflect." *Selah* was also used as a musical notation understood by musicians as "interlude," especially as the word appears as such in thirty-nine of the psalms, including three times in the third Psalm, which David composed concerning the time he fled from his son Absalom.

> LORD, how are they increased that trouble me!
>> many are they that rise up against me.
> Many there be which say of my soul, There is no help
>> for him in God. *Selah*.
> But thou, O LORD, art a shield for me; my glory, and
>> the lifter up of mine head.
> I cried unto the LORD with my voice, and he heard
>> me out of his holy hill. *Selah*.
> I laid me down and slept; I awaked; for the LORD
>> sustained me.
> I will not be afraid of ten thousands of people, that
>> have set themselves against me round about.
> Arise, O LORD; save me, O my God: for thou hast
>> smitten all mine enemies upon the cheek bone;
>> thou hast broken the teeth of the ungodly.
> Salvation belongeth unto the LORD: thy blessing is
>> upon thy people. *Selah*.

(Psalm 3 KJV)

Selah is usually directed to the choirmaster and appears at the end of the psalm. I like to think of these three pauses in Psalm 3 as *one for the Father, one for the Son, and one for the Holy Spirit*. And in my "sanctified imagination" (as preachers like to say), I translate *selah* as this God-directive to David:

"David, *stop* singing your psalms, *stop* playing your harp . . . for a moment. Pause, reflect, *rest*, and enjoy what you've just played. Let it be music to your ears. . . . You've come to the end of your song, the end of your day. Now rest. It's all right. Give yourself permission to even stop. You now need to hear *my* voice, as I've heard yours throughout this day."

That's the kind of call to rest familiar to me. I've come to relish a retreat event I created and call *Selah by the Sea*, and other downtime gatherings with God, organized to reintroduce rest and reflection for me and sisters from all over the world, including many who have contributed to this devotional book. Restful reflection times have become part of our lives. We drop work—literally—gather for refreshment and recuperation, and experience spiritual and physical renewal.

Peaceful pauses were introduced to me in childhood. Rest was reinforced with visits to my grandmother's house in Concord, North Carolina, especially during summertime when "the living is easy." The annual ritual for kids born in the North was for our Southern parents to send us *down South*. We city kids got away from the busy streets and fast life of New York, or whichever urban community we found ourselves in.

With maturity and wisdom, I now realize our parents were giving us the best break of our lives. "When I was a child, . . .

I thought as a child; . . . but when I became a [wo]man, I put away childish things (1 Corinthians 13:11 NKJV).

These summers taught us to mandate rest. In the slowing down with extended family, some major refreshing happened for us, and for our parents. There was such deep appreciation for simply *life*. Not the fast life. We saw our elders take their time. They didn't cram too much into any day. And they allowed time to revisit the most important and sacred element of life: being with God, and God alone.

During those summer visits in the country, all the first, second, and third cousins in a certain age-group stayed with Mama, my maternal grandmother. We were all raised together as the children of sisters, brothers, and very close cousins. That's how our parents kept us, together, like brothers and sisters. All summer long, when the "grands" would get on Mama's last, good Christian nerve, or when we were moving too fast because we still had that city energy, she'd exclaim, "Sit down and rest your nerves!"

In the Holy Scriptures, I imagine that's how God translates *selah* for us: *Sit down and rest. Rest your nerves. Let your mind, body, and spirit catch up with one another and with me. In fact, let me catch you, capture you, arrest you with my Holy Spirit.*

God calls us to reflective, sacred time. Moments when nothing moves us but Him. Do you recall the moment when you first truly knew you were God's child? When you stopped and said, "Lord, I'm yours"?

At this writing, it seems God has called the whole world to pause in the worst reported crisis of our lifetime, a pandemic. The world literally slowed almost to a standstill—economically, medically, physically, and I dare say, spiritually. We need to pause and *turn toward* the light. Not *the light at the end of the tunnel*, but Jesus, the Light of the world.

> If my people, who are called by my name,
> will humble themselves and pray and seek my
> face and turn from their wicked ways, then I
> will hear from heaven, and I will forgive their
> sin and heal their land. (2 Chronicles 7:14)

Sister Evelyn Miller-Suber was the first to notice that we could scramble the letters *s-e-l-a-h* to spell the word *heals*. Selah time is a seeking-God's-face healing time. It seems to me God's Earth can burn out physically, economically, morally, ethically, and spiritually. And I know about burnout.

I accepted God's call into the ministry at the young age of twenty-three. While still in seminary, at the age of twenty-six, I was elected to become pastor of a historic church in New York City, my hometown. I was excited. They were excited to have me. But we ran off adrenaline and emotion until one day, with no boundaries, a packed schedule, and limited resources, I burned out.

If you don't know what burnout feels like, let me describe it: You *have* a job, but don't want to *go* to the job. You *wake* up, but you don't feel like *getting* up. You have a calendar *filled* with appointments, but you don't know if you'll *make* it until lunchtime. Burnout is *real*. It does not feel good. As a young woman pastoring in the inner city—the demands and needs were greater than my human ability to meet them. I was *driven* to a Spirit-led rest.

When I finally stopped and looked around to catch up with myself and reflected on the blessings of my labor, so many of my trailblazing sisters with whom I had embarked on this new journey of ministry—my co-sojourners, especially clergy-women—had fallen prey to burnout, and some were actually gone. They had passed away, or they were very ill, or joyless. And the psalm came to me: "How shall we sing the LORD's song in a strange land?" (137:4 KJV). It was a strained and strange time.

Women entering the ministry didn't know how or where it was safe to stop. It took so long to *get in* the positions, and to get to the "stained-glass" tables, and to break through stained-glass ceilings. Many feared that pausing would stir up and ignite politics. Others might attempt to position themselves in the interim or take over women's spots, even if only for a day. So we worked nonstop, and instead of *shopping till we dropped*, we were simply not stopping or shopping, and then we just dropped. Burned out.

That's why, for about twenty years, I've invited a group of Christian women to gather, to sojourn together for a few days each fall to reintroduce stopping. I challenge women to slow down, to pause, and to get away with God. So that *it is well* with our soul, as the hymnist confessed. My ministry has become one of wholeness and wellness: wellness in our spirit, wellness in our mind, wellness in our work, and wellness in our rest. So that we women have what the Holy Bible describes as souls that *prosper* (3 John 2). So in my endeavors, I advise that we women slow down, pause, and move away . . .

Away from the trials, toils, and tolls of trailblazing;

away from the critics, the cynics, and the conflict;

away from the politics and pandemics;

away, we leap into our Father's lap.

Lean on His everlasting arms,

learn to rest from the stress, mess, and tests;

lie down in spiritual and literal leisure;

jump into joy; sail into selah.

When we pause, we experience solace for our souls, hope for our hurts, and healing restoration. Wherever we are, we all can find spiritual space to pause and reflect, and listen to our heavenly Parent. We need to engage in rhythms of rest, and as we do, we also develop bonds of sisterhood. We're blessed to share with our sisters in these devotions and stories about living and listening and overcoming, about taking time with and resting in God, even as we're women on the move together.

Sister, I personally invite you to put on your spiritual dancing shoes and attend the Holy Ghost party awaiting you in the pages of this devotional. May these pages *pop* in your heart, put pep in your spiritual step, and give pizzazz, joy, and peaceful rest in your soul. May this book be your spiritual rite of passage, as you give yourself permission to experience *Rhythms of Rest*.

—*Suzan D. Johnson Cook*

Water will gush forth

in the wilderness

and streams in the desert.

ISAIAH 35:6

Spirit-Led Moves

Renowned author Langston Hughes once said, "Life for [us] ain't been no crystal stair." Let me put it this way: life has not been an easy stroll in the park; life has had its share of tears, snares in it, wear and tear on it, tacks in it, times we wanted to turn back in it. But we wholeheartedly concur, *God is good all the time*! I've found that if I can bask in the Lord—no matter where I find myself—I can cope. Perhaps that's part of what the apostle Paul meant when he said, "I have learned to be content, whatever the circumstances" (Philippians 4:11). I've lived long enough to know that God does not fail: "He who began a good work in you will carry it on to completion" (Philippians 1:6). Even when I have felt as though I am passing through a wilderness.

I've discovered *wilderness* to be circumstances and spaces between where we *were* and where God is taking us. It's not haphazard but is a "seasoning" space—where God seasons us with His presence, His love, all of himself—that can take us far beyond reasoning. Because God doesn't call us to simply have clarity and be comfortable. God calls us to be faithful and, when we are, our lives and our service to others become remarkable. In the wilderness, we don't always *feel* comfortable because we aren't in control; God is. Yet that is exactly what *Spirit-led* living is all about.

And I've discovered that there is rest—even in the wilderness. God does not limit our spiritual rest in Him to a particular day, time, way, environment, or circumstance. We can rest in God in a wilderness. When we examine Jesus's life and ministry, we see that Jesus was *led* by the Spirit—driven by the Spirit—into the wilderness before beginning His earthly ministry (Luke 4). God, on purpose and with purpose, planned for Jesus to experience a time of testing and proving—alone—away from everything and everyone. Jesus found His rest in God and God's words and plans.

Remember the children of Israel as they were fleeing Egypt, en route to the Promised Land? They, too, were led to wilderness. That's where Moses developed his best leadership style, because he had to stop and listen to God, depend on the God who commanded and demanded that His people be set free. Moses encountered disgust, dismay, disrespect, division, uncertainty, and agitation (Exodus 13–14). The people he led were afraid of being taken away from the familiar, though the familiar was oppressive. On this journey of liberation, Moses also experienced confirmation, hope, and a word of salvation in direct communication with God by the Red Sea. God knew all Moses would encounter, including when he got to the other side. Moses was developing what I call "frontline faith," the faith and fortitude needed for God to do some of His best work in us.

How about us? What happens for sisters waiting in our wildernesses? When we pause, even stop by the "Red Seas" of our lives, we receive confirmations from God too. We get enough strength and faith in the midst of whatever we're going through as we reflect on Him and His Word. In our wilderness experiences—like Jesus's and Israel's—we can keep going. We can overcome and get to the other side as we listen to God.

We cannot avoid our wilderness experiences, which are often Spirit-led. Jesus stood on God's every word (Matthew 4:4; Luke 4:4). Moses listened when God told him to tell the people to go forward on their journey (Exodus 14:16, 21).

We sisters are going forward, even as we face frontline issues and crises. Solo as well as together with other sisters, armed with faith, we receive the blessed gift of time with God that empowers each of us to face times that demand frontline faith.

It's interesting COVID-19 surfaced prominently in the United States in 2020, just before spring. The pandemic continued with us during the months leading up to Easter, the season of Lent, when we are to draw closer to the cross, to Jesus. While at the time of editing this book, the terminology has continued to be *keep a social distance*, staying farther apart, away from one another as we walk down the street or carefully meet. That has never meant keeping a *spiritual* distance. God's Spirit always allows us to draw close—closer to God, closer to Jesus on the cross—as we follow His path. Closer to one another in Christ. Spirit-led, the cross was Jesus's wilderness and agony He gladly accepted for us, that we might walk closer with Him and each other.

—*Suzan D. Johnson Cook*

First Steps

But those who trust in the Lord will find new strength.
They will soar high on wings like eagles.
They will run and not grow weary.
They will walk and not faint.

ISAIAH 40:31 (NLT)

*W*hat motivates babies to take their first steps—to get up, and to walk? They reach their little hand up for something to hold onto, pull themselves up to stand, and attempt a few unsteady steps. Toppling and plopping repeatedly, something inside them tells them to try again and again until they're stepping confidently. Likewise, what motivates us to try again to live our best lives? The Holy Spirit.

God moves us to take our first step and stand as new believers, and guides our every step during our years of traveling this life. We may not know every road we will walk or the number of steps it will take to get to our destination. One step at time, God gives us firm footing to succeed. He reminds us need not worry about living in a corrupt, evil world when we're confronted with difficulties and detours. We're promised, "The Lord makes firm the steps of the one who delights in him; though he may stumble, he will not fall, for the Lord upholds him with his hand" (Psalm 37:23–24).

It pleases God when we seek Him for guidance and help along life's many detours and reverses in course. When we need to regain our footing and keep walking toward our goals, God reminds us that those who trust in Him will find new strength (see Isaiah 40:28–31). The prophet Isaiah's words tell us that in desperate times we can rest and trust in God so our strength can be restored and renewed. We are reminded God is at every turn on life's winding, low or high road. When we purposely commune with God, through the Holy Spirit, we are empowered to keep stepping. And the Holy Spirit inspires us to stop, pray, and commune with God.

The Holy Spirit knows the number of our steps and when we are weary or uncertain. Every time we feel tired or fear falling, the Holy Spirit is there to inspire and encourage us to get back up again.

As you walk through life, remember the Holy Spirit was there when you took your first step. God's Holy Spirit is still available when you step into problems and need a way out. God can help you sidestep problems and reposition your steps with resolve, to accomplish your goals and life mission.

Reflection

How many steps have you taken since you purposely communed with God?

• • •

How has the Holy Spirit inspired you to share your journey with others so the knowledge and wisdom you've gained can be multiplied to others' benefit?

Isaiah 40:28–31 (NKJV)

²⁸ Have you not known?
Have you not heard?
The everlasting God, the LORD,
The Creator of the ends of the earth,
Neither faints nor is weary.
His understanding is unsearchable.
²⁹ He gives power to the weak,
And to those who have no might He increases strength.
³⁰ Even the youths shall faint and be weary,
And the young men shall utterly fall,
³¹ But those who wait on the LORD
Shall renew their strength;
They shall mount up with wings like eagles,
They shall run and not be weary,
They shall walk and not faint.

Come, Let's Go

When Jesus saw the crowd around him,
he gave orders to cross to the other side of the lake.

MATTHEW 8:18

*L*ord, I need help today! My plate is full, and I haven't even gotten out of bed! My mind raced between commitments: *I have to visit the sick in the hospital; I have to help with a funeral; I need to sit down with a member and her daughter; and attend a community meeting. Oh, and I need to prepare my sermon. And make phone calls, send texts, and emails.*

I also need to remember to hydrate . . . and when do I listen to the Lord? This was a typical day for me in ministry, not just for a year but for years. And it left me depleted.

I had to learn to answer the call to pause, to listen in God's presence, to experience necessary learning and refreshing relationships in retreat alone and with others. Pain was a motivating factor for me to embrace these practices. Doing a lot—or should I say too much—has taken great physical toll on me over my years in ministry. Sometimes my family thinks I still do too much. But I've also learned to respond to the call to selah. To "be there" in retreat—as one great mentor pointed out to me. And thankfully, another of my mentors had advised me to set aside some of the financial offerings I received as a preacher to use for essentials. Retreating with God is essential.

When we look at Scripture, we see that Jesus thought so too. He needed to get away. He needed to take time out. So He did, even amid ministry. We see Jesus teaching, preaching, taking care of His close relationships, and performing so many healing miracles. But at the right time, even Jesus told those following alongside Him to stop. "Come let's go over to the other side," Jesus said. He made His disciples travel in a boat to the other side of the sea. He knew they needed to rest and to get away from the crowds. One time, Jesus rested in a boat on the sea before calming the storm and casting out more demons (Matthew 8:24–32).

Sisters, we, too, must get away! We multitask, take care of everyone but ourselves, and really do it all—in our home, in our churches, at work. Rarely do we spend time on ourselves. Some of us have missed our own birthdays. We look up at the end of our days and say, Where has the time gone? And, God, what did I miss? When we can study the Bible, treat ourselves royally with rest, bask in new relationships, receive support from other women, speak about our feelings, . . . let's do so. Spending this time with God alone or in fellowship with others gives us the needed push, or oomph, to do even greater things in our own lives and communities.

When we hear Jesus's call to "come, let's go to the other side"—the invitation to selah—it's time to draw near to our Savior.

Time to be blessed as we interact with God. To be with sisters who know and understand. Sisters who will listen, letting us share our hearts. Sisters, who hear us out without criticizing. Sisters who can talk and learn from one another. Just sisters who are servants of the living God, helping each other.

Reminding ourselves of our calling and the gifts that God has given us—encouraging us to stay the course.

Oh, to sit and listen. Oh, how He speaks and brings so much to remembrance. Think about how God has taken care of you, blessed you with your job, calling, assignment, or season of life, keeping you through it all, inspiring new approaches to so many things. Come, let us sit in awe and listen intensely. What a blessing.

Reflection

How do you spend selah time?

• • •

Is it now time to sleep, pamper yourself, listen, and spend uninterrupted time with the Lord?

Psalm 4 (*NKJV*)

> [1] Hear me when I call, O God of my righteousness!
> You have relieved me in my distress;
> Have mercy on me, and hear my prayer.
>
> [2] How long, O you sons of men,
> Will you turn my glory to shame?
> How long will you love worthlessness
> And seek falsehood? *Selah*
> [3] But know that the LORD has set apart for Himself him
>   who is godly;

The LORD will hear when I call to Him.

⁴ Be angry, and do not sin.
Meditate within your heart on your bed, and be still. *Selah*
⁵ Offer the sacrifices of righteousness,
And put your trust in the LORD.

⁶ There are many who say,
"Who will show us any good?"
LORD, lift up the light of Your countenance upon us.
⁷ You have put gladness in my heart,
More than in the season that their grain and wine
　　　　　increased.
⁸ I will both lie down in peace, and sleep;
For You alone, O LORD, make me dwell in safety.

An Invitation

Take off your sandals,
for the place where you are standing
is holy ground.

EXODUS 3:5

In the middle of producing a major citywide event—something I've done time and time again—the invitation to take selah, a personal retreat, came. Overwhelmed with all of the moving parts of that year's "Empowerment Project," I really needed to take a breather for myself. But my only refreshing times had been in my fifteen- to thirty-minute "power sighs" in the confines of my office with the lights out and the door closed.

The invitation to rest—just the sound of it—was relaxing. *This is not the time*, my mind argued back. *How dare I take time away to fly out of the city for days at this critical point of the production? So much depends on my being present.*

But, oh, how I wished that I could step away. My soul needed it. I felt, though, the project needed me more. *I can wait, and, maybe at the end, there will be enough energy left for me to simply breathe*, I told myself.

Burning within, however, was the invitation to follow the Voice speaking to my heart. I raised every consideration and objection as to why it was not the right time. *I can't retreat now. How would it look? My chief executive officer would object with the deadlines fast approaching. The vendors, sponsors, speakers, venue, caterers, teams—all need me to be here. How can I not? I can't and I won't.*

I felt a voice of encouragement arise. I imagined Moses's response when given the invitation to do what his mind had cried out for: the liberation of his people. And God, making use of Moses's desire, called out to him, telling him to go and what to do, step by step. Many were Moses's considerations and varied were his objections as to why he could not and should not go (Exodus 3:6–11; 4:1–17). But God called! I heard: *You have already oiled all of the pieces and parts of this project; the event will run without you.*

God has a way of showing us our worth, value, capabilities, and His plans for us when we stop and listen to Him— even when we can't see them or understand our worth and resist following and resting in Him. There is something about the encouraging Voice of God that burns in our heart until we say, *Yes, I can and I must follow God.* As we learn to trust God and follow His Voice, we begin to realize God's plans surpass our conflicting considerations. As the all-knowing, all-powerful One, He makes a way for us to follow Him, no matter how challenging the circumstances. In fact, all our hopes and dreams depend on what He has planned for us

God has more for us than what we see from where we stand. Give yourself permission to accept the invitation to pause, listen, and rest with God. Every other consideration will be handled, and every objection overruled by God, who has purposely designed moments for selah. Concessions will be made, paving the way, freeing you from all constraints. Retreat with God. Selah!

Exodus 3:13–17 (NLT)

[13] But Moses protested, "If I go to the people of Israel and tell them, 'The God of your ancestors has sent me to you,' they will ask me, 'What is his name?' Then what should I tell them?"

[14] God replied to Moses, "I AM WHO I AM. Say this to the people of Israel: I AM has sent me to you." [15] God also said to Moses, "Say this to the people of Israel: Yahweh, the God of your ancestors—the God of Abraham, the God of Isaac, and the God of Jacob—has sent me to you.

> This is my eternal name,
> my name to remember for all generations.

[16] "Now go and call together all the elders of Israel. Tell them, 'Yahweh, the God of your ancestors—the God of Abraham, Isaac, and Jacob—has appeared to me. He told me, "I

Reflection

God calls us to action, but He also invites us to pause: to enter the fullness of listening to His divine plans and aligning with them. In retreat with others or alone, we are liberated and empowered by spending time in His holy presence. How will you respond?

have been watching closely, and I see how the Egyptians are treating you. ¹⁷ I have promised to rescue you from your oppression in Egypt. I will lead you to a land flowing with milk and honey.'"

Joy Dances

He has enabled us to be ministers of his new covenant.
This is a covenant not of written laws, but of the Spirit.
The old written covenant ends in death;
but under the new covenant, the Spirit gives life.

2 CORINTHIANS 3:6 (NLT)

Worshiping the Lord, I gaily moved my feet, enraptured by the power that engulfed me. A fleeting thought from the distant past attempted to abort this beautiful experience. *Dancing is worldly; it's not of God. You could go to hell for this.* At that instant, the grip on my worship flag tightened, causing it to soar higher and more vigorously, sweeping away that haunting voice. A sweeter, gentle voice beckoned me, *Come, . . . come, my beloved.* Responding to this invitation, I sensed myself in the embrace of the loving arms of my heavenly Father.

Moments like these are the epitome of joy—to be swept away in the Spirit through the worship of dance. I cherish these moments because for years religious constraints had stifled my creative expressions through movement. The religious tradition that my mother embraced had taught me as a child that dancing is worldly, sensual, and inappropriate for a Christian.

Therefore, this precious gift of dance had been dormant within me, buried beneath legalism.

In an attempt to find the peace, comfort, and joy that I experienced through dance, I would steal away on personal retreats and search my heart through prayer, Scripture reading, and meditation. While communing with nature, observing the swaying of the trees, the fluttering of the birds, the glistening and quaking flowers, and the thrashing of the ocean, God drew me closer, as though I were in motion with Him. Oh, how I longed to dance.

Sadness and confusion were replacing the joy I had once experienced through the dance. Living under the inhibitions of religiosity, my body submitted to this lifestyle, but my spirit was in a state of oscillation. I could not settle with the idea that living in bondage to rules is what God requires of us as His people.

God is faithful! The light turned on while I sat in a systematic theology class that revived my soul. As the professor explained, "We no longer live under the old covenant that kills, but the new covenant that gives life," my mind reveled in the truth: *So Christ has truly set us free. Now make sure that you stay free, and don't get tied up again in slavery to the law* (Galatians 5:1 NLT).

Wow! Life is meant to be lived in the Spirit and not by the letter of the law. Hallelujah! The hope, joy, and peace that I had been yearning for flooded my being. My spirit leaped and the healing balm of God's love washed over me and began to restore my soul. I wanted to run and tell the world, *I can dance . . . I can dance!*

This moment was a golden game changer, a lifeline. God redeemed me, to again express my innermost being freely through the movement of my body. Slowly, I learned to dance again and to embrace the accompanying joy.

Now, when I take time to retreat, I am no longer an observer of nature's movements. I'm a participant; I have become a dancing partner. Whether I'm interacting with nature, fellowshiping with like-minded sisters, or sequestered in my home, I can dance with abandon. All of it empowers me for the next steps in life.

Being led by the Spirit opens us up to endless possibilities. And so I dance with joy.

I have found the joy of living free in Christ, and you can too. Don't be bewitched by man-made rules.

Reflection

What parts of your ministry assignment and calling from God do you still struggle with in your own strength?

* * *

When you allow the Spirit to lead you, what happens?

Romans 8:1–6

[1] Therefore, there is now no condemnation for those who are in Christ Jesus, [2] because through Christ Jesus the law of the Spirit who gives life has set you free from the law of sin and death. [3] For what the law was powerless to do because it was weakened by the flesh, God did by sending his own Son in the likeness of sinful flesh to be a sin offering. And so he condemned sin in the

flesh, [4] in order that the righteous requirement of the law might be fully met in us, who do not live according to the flesh but according to the Spirit.

[5] Those who live according to the flesh have their minds set on what the flesh desires; but those who live in accordance with the Spirit have their minds set on what the Spirit desires. [6] The mind governed by the flesh is death, but the mind governed by the Spirit is life and peace.

A Brand-New Beginning

I am the vine; you are the branches.
If you remain in me and I in you, you will bear much fruit;
apart from me you can do nothing.

JOHN 15:5

In the spring, I began noticing an emptiness in my life. I began getting frustrated during my daily activities and was clueless as to why. After all, *I'm living a pretty good life,* I thought. *I am an entrepreneur, happily married, living in a beautiful new home, my kids are thriving in school, . . . and I just purchased a new BMW convertible.* Everything seemed to be working in my favor as far as I could see at the time. But deep inside, I felt something missing. It was God!

One afternoon while feeling lonely and frustrated, I sensed the voice of the Lord ask, *Where is your Bible?* His voice felt audible to me, as though God was standing right next to me. I recall gasping and covering my mouth. "Where is my Bible?" I asked myself aloud.

After hearing the voice of the Lord that day, I began keeping the Word close to me, reading my Bible daily. I started in the book of John. While studying, I began to cry. Not only did reading the gospel of John educate me on the life of Christ; it made me take a candid look in the mirror, at my life. Evaluating my spiritual condition, comparing it to the Holy Scriptures—I was devastated. I had never before *truly* evaluated my life according to the Word. You see, I considered myself a Christian, but I was not *abiding* in Him (John 15:5). I was spiritually bankrupt of His will for my life. I knew right then I needed to change, reverse course, repent.

I began changing my daily habits. Each day, before doing anything else, I pursued spending one-on-one time with God, reading my Bible and praying. After about ninety days of renewing my mind with the truths in God's Word, I started to see a change. I started seeing life from a different perspective. I remember praying this simple commitment: "God, take people out of my life that aren't supposed to be there, and surround me with people who are."

Shortly after that, I began attending Christian women's conferences too. One year, while attending a conference in Maryland, I heard a woman on stage speaking boldly about the things of God. She communicated with such confidence and seemed to be happy and very secure with her message. I thought, *Wow. She's fearless!* The following year, I attended the same conference and connected with its leadership. Shortly after, I began meeting more amazing, Spirit-led leaders from all over the world. I also became a participant in online courses that inspired me to share my faith with others on a deeper level and in a broader way.

I have found that when we abide in God's Word, it transforms our hearts and directs our will for God's glory. Learning to discern the voice of the Lord can and will change the trajectory of our lives. God always has a way of positioning us right where He wants us to be. Now, I am committed to encouraging others to abide in Christ, His love, and His Word. I now understand what I was missing was a true relationship with God built on the understanding of God's Word. While I had everything in life I thought I wanted, there was indeed more—and it was God and learning to abide in Him.

John 15:1–5 (NKJV)

[1] "I am the true vine, and My Father is the vinedresser. [2] Every branch in Me that does not bear fruit He takes away; and every branch that bears fruit He prunes, that it may bear more fruit. [3] You are already clean because of the word which I have spoken to you. [4] Abide in Me, and I in you. As the branch cannot bear fruit of itself, unless it abides in the vine, neither can you, unless you abide in Me.

[5] "I am the vine, you are the branches. He who abides in Me, and I in him, bears much fruit; for without Me you can do nothing."

Reflection

Which passages of the Bible have spoken to you personally?

*Blessed be the L*ORD*,*

Who daily loads us

with benefits,

The God of our salvation!

Selah

PSALM 68:19 (NKJV)

Self-Care
Steps

*W*omen are servant leaders who are so busy caring for others that it sometimes feels abnormal to carve out time for ourselves. But Scripture tells us we have a choice. Jesus declared, "I have come that [you] may have life, and that [you] may have it more abundantly" (John 10:10 NKJV). Part of that abundance includes enjoying solitary time with the Lord and the pure joy that can come from rest with God. Because our self-care matters.

When I invite women to my retreats, we enjoy a combination of self-care, friendship time, and leadership development. This is not business as usual. It's full of moments for making what's not the norm the norm—being proactive for health in body and soul, rather than reactive to crises. For me, retreat is a part of the abundant life Jesus promised us—the after-caring-for-your-kids, your-parents, your-spouse, and your-work abundant life.

That means first and foremost leaning into these words from the Lord: "And thou shalt love the Lord thy God with all thy heart, and with all thy soul, and with all thy mind, and with all thy strength: this is the first commandment. And the second is like, namely this, Thou shalt love thy neighbour *as thyself.* There is none other commandment greater than these" (Mark 12:30–31 KJV; emphasis added).

We cannot pour out anything more, anywhere, or into anyone else if we don't show loving care to ourselves. Sometimes we must be taught—and then see—this modeled. Other times, we simply need to be reminded. Sometimes self-care means saying no or not now. Other times it means intentional planning for and choosing a lounge chair poolside. Or retreating to a comfy chair in a corner, all alone, at home. Asking someone else to cook our eggs sunny-side up. Or bringing our fried selves to the sunshine and sea or another relaxing activity.

At Selah by the Sea, there's a rhythm to the retreat that emphasizes pause. We intentionally include what we call M.U.S.H. time to unwind and listen to God. You can practice M.U.S.H. time with others at an organized retreat such as Selah by the Sea, or adapt the concept to your home front, or any other place you might be able to get away to, if only for a moment:

> Massage
> Umbrella (hide away under one, or any space that allows you to relax)
> Sit, sleep, siesta.
> Holy hush time . . . embrace it.

God shows us that all of nature has an on and off time.

Nature is commanded to take a time-out. The Creator calls us to pause too. Even waves have a selah. They don't splash all day long. Their intensity slows long enough to smooth out the sand. Pick up an empty seashell cast onto the shore, and put it to your ear, and you'll hear sounds amplify. Emptying our schedules and opening our hearts gives place and space to hear God fully. We can trade in our briefcases for bathing suits, and fancy high heels for flip-flops. We can take time to get into the rhythms of God's universe—ebb and flow, movement and rest.

By the second or third day of our retreats, we realize there's absolutely nothing wrong with wearing no makeup. In fact, it's good every now and then to let your skin breathe and to let your hair get some air, to let your waistline smile wide, and to let your toes get some sand in between them. To giggle hysterically and play hide-and-seek in the waters. To gaze awhile at the sunrises and the sunsets God paints with His favorite colors kissing the sky.

Wherever you are, take a moment to realize we matter as much as those we appreciate and serve, lead, and provide caregiving to. And that self-care is equally important—that we are important to God. We are His daughters. Spend time wondering, sometimes wandering, but always make space for unwinding. Be reminded that "the race is not to the swift, nor the battle to the strong," but to the one who endures (Ecclesiastes 9:11 KJV). Selah helps us endure. And take care of ourselves.

In my role as a religious freedom ambassador, I learned a definition of freedom, especially religious freedom. It's when people can bring their whole lives, fully and freely—bring their authentic selves to work, to worship, to work out, and to play.

In Exodus 15:1–8, we read about Miriam, Moses, and all the leaders dancing on the other side of the Red Sea. I believe they realized: this is what real freedom feels like, looks like, tastes like. It is getting to the other side, including the other side of pain, fatigue, depression, loneliness, isolation, doubt. Getting to the other side where your spirit says, Yes, I'm leaping and dancing: I'm alive.

We are called to be stewards over all the earth, and to take care of ourselves. God mandates us to care for the fish, for the fowl, for every living thing, and that includes ourselves. Nothing and no one should distract us from being God's best, and remembering His command, "Love thy neighbor as thyself." But somewhere along the way, the concept of *taking care of self* has been misinterpreted.

Self-care enables us to give more to others. Some trailblazing women feel they are too busy to take care of themselves, to deal with their own needs. They would rather deposit and pour themselves into others. Yet, this can become detrimental to their health. According to many reports, many burn out, suffer depression, and are stressed. (Add that equation or formula to Black, Indigenous, People of Color women, and the numbers are exponentially higher.) Many are burned out, tired out, worn out, all the while trying to gain entry to a system that constantly tries to keep them out. Nothing that is depleted is helpful for those who need to be completed. Soul singer Billy Preston reminded in his pop song, "Nothin' from nothin' leaves nothin'."

I believe God is crying out to us: *Bring yourselves, even with your emptiness, and let me fill you, let me care for you.* God placed twenty-four hours in a day. We need to use our time wisely, including when we stop doing. What do you do when you stop doing? I love the water. Water brings me life. Being near it, wading in it, swimming in it, watching it. I've rediscovered my love for swimming, and I literally can stay in water all day.

When my brother and I were young teens, our parents took us to Puerto Rico. It was a big deal, leaving the Bronx and going to the islands. For several summers, we'd stay at Condado Beach. Our parents would book a two-week stay. Well, my brother and I would stay at the hotel when our parents went on sightseeing tours. When they left for one, I was in the pool, and when they came back several hours later, there I'd be, still in the pool. The pool remains one of my favorite things.

When I can, it's such a joy to be in the pool with my sisters. One doesn't have to swim. Just splash, and that's enough. It's salve for the soul. But my self-care menu doesn't wait to start until I can get to water. It has "appetizers, entrées, and dessert," a full-course meal. For me, self-care is a lifestyle with several components.

A commercial recently caught my eye when it used this tagline to promote a new car model, "It's where my new life meets my new lifestyle." Selah allows us to be that new model on God's assembly line. If you've ever gone to or seen a car manufacturing plant, maybe in Detroit, Michigan, you will see there are different stations. One person puts the bumper on, another goes under the hood, another places the battery in, another attaches the upholstery, and one shines up the new model when it's ready. All year long, we're being assembled, tested. Our "nuts and bolts" have come loose and need to be tightened. Then there's retreat time—whether personal or with our sisters—when our parts come together, we pause, and then we can go and flow. That's what *selah* means to me: a place and space that allows us to discover and uncover our needs, where we can get our flow. We must always pay attention to self-care, making it our lifestyle. Pledge with me that you'll take care of yourself—as a lifestyle.

—*Suzan D. Johnson Cook*

Comforted by Christ

He refreshes my soul.

PSALM 23:3

It's Monday morning, and I get a Zoom invite from a writer's group. They're hosting a lunchtime get-together. But as I read the email, I shake my head no. No, to another Zoom call. No, to an awkward group chat. No, in a sad time of pandemic, to a tough time of sharing pain. Instead, *May I take a break, O Lord? A break with You?*

Humbled by my questions, I dare to ask God for His help. Especially for my "self." As I wrote this, indeed, a family friend became sick with COVID-19, and just one day later, that friend died. *So, what of my own self-care? Does it truly matter?*

I weigh such burdens because I'd misunderstood self-care. I'd thought it meant yoga, massages, and turning off my phone sooner every day. All good things. But where was my *self* in that care? In truth, on a yoga mat, my *self* got lost.

Then came the pandemic. For restoration, I turned to God—discovering what? First, He calls us with ease and perfect compassion: "Come to me, all you who are weary and burdened, and I will give you rest" (Matthew 11:28).

In that rest, the Lord teaches us of His nature, but also

about ourselves—especially how we can find our *self*, personally, in His rest. As He tells us, "meditate in your heart" and "be still," in Psalm 4:4 (NASB). In that way, the Lord reveals our own distinct triggers for fatigue, fear, sin, anger, loneliness, but also our own strengths.

With self-awareness, then, we find rest in His presence and peace. So, I remember my introverted needs—not for yoga or massage, but first for Him. As Psalm 4 concludes, "Selah" (v. 4). Or, as David declared in the Twenty-third Psalm, "*He* refreshes my soul" (v. 3; emphasis added).

So, my Zoom call? *Cancel it*, He answers. Then? *Follow me. Learn from me.* So, there I go, landing not in calm, but in the churning sixth chapter of the gospel of Mark. Our Selah Jesus has already healed a man of his demon, raised Jairus's daughter from the dead, and restored the woman with the issue of blood—all in chapter five. Now in six, He's rejected by His hometown, yet He sends out His disciples, endures John the Baptist's beheading, feeds five thousand famished village men and their families—*and* walks on storm-tossed water.

Then, Jesus offers a remarkable gift of self-care. As He told His wearied disciples, "Come with me by yourselves to a quiet place and get some rest" (Mark 6:31). He and the Twelve hadn't even had time to eat. Led by Jesus, however, "they went away by themselves in a boat to a solitary place" (v. 32).

It's a stunning portrait of self-care. Get alone with God. In a quiet place. Then, in His presence, graced by His Spirit, He tends to our souls. Personally. As David proclaimed, "He makes me lie down in green pastures, he leads me beside quiet waters (Psalm 23:2). And if you've ever seen a roiling steam suddenly go still, be assured it is resting over a deep, deep place.

In Christ, our deep place is our Lord.

Thus, I find Him in His Word. Reading a psalm or a gospel story or a battle victory, I feel my battle-worn soul revive. David did too. "Even though I walk through the darkest valley . . . you are with me," comforting (Psalm 23:4).

Reflection

As you answer the Lord's call to rest, what do you learn about yourself— and how you best rest in Him??

And *that* is self-care. Comforted by God who knows us and never leaves. Selah.

Lord, call my name before I run off to manage my self-care—drawing me instead to You.

Mark 6:6–13, 30–32

6 Then Jesus went around teaching from village to village. 7 Calling the Twelve to him, he began to send them out two by two and gave them authority over impure spirits.

8 These were his instructions: "Take nothing for the journey except a staff—no bread, no bag, no money in your belts. 9 Wear sandals but not an extra shirt. 10 Whenever you enter a house, stay there until you leave that town. 11 And if any place will not welcome you or listen to you, leave that place and shake the dust off your feet as a testimony against them."

12 They went out and preached that people should repent. 13 They drove out many demons and anointed many sick people with oil and healed them. . . .

[30] The apostles gathered around Jesus and reported to him all they had done and taught. [31] Then, because so many people were coming and going that they did not even have a chance to eat, he said to them, "Come with me by yourselves to a quiet place and get some rest."

[32] So they went away by themselves in a boat to a solitary place.

Everyone Is Looking for You

Very early in the morning, while it was still dark,
Jesus got up, left the house and went off to a solitary place,
where he prayed. Simon and his companions went to look for him,
and when they found him, they exclaimed:
"Everyone is looking for you!"

MARK 1:35–37

I must admit that I fell out laughing when I read verse 37 in the first chapter of Mark's gospel. I envisioned Simon and his companions in a state of panic when they could not find Jesus; and then in a serious state of relief when they finally found Him up on a mountain spending time in prayer. They exclaimed, "Everyone is looking for you!"

Even though my context is completely different, it reminded me of times when I need some solo time. Like when I go out and away from my family for some "me time" and get my nails and hair done. As soon as I get home, my children will be at the door waiting for me and saying, "Mommy, where were you?" Mind you, they did not need anything; they just needed to know I was there in the house with them!

Interestingly, Jesus's closest disciples did not realize that Jesus needed some selah and prayer time with his Father. They had expected Him to be present with them. And did they think Jesus would be at their beck and call every moment of the day? After all, in the verses leading up to verse 37, Jesus had just finished healing Simon's mother-in-law and many others; and He had to cast out demons! What next?

There are going to be times in our lives when we feel that everyone is looking for us, seeking our attention and presence simultaneously. The kids will be calling every few minutes for us to do something, which we cannot ignore or deny. A mate may be desiring attention and expecting a suitable response. The people we lead in ministry will be anxiously waiting for our next move, our next word we've heard from God, our next event, and so on. There will also be times in our professional work where all eyes will be on us to go higher and to produce, produce, and produce some more.

So, before the search party goes out looking for us, it's important that we prepare ourselves to do what God has equipped and assigned us to do. Prepare ourselves by going to our place of solitude. When we go there, we can get our mind right. Pray. Focus. Recharge. Refuel. Relax. Remind ourselves that we are a marvelous mom, a wonderful wife, a powerful preacher, a moving missionary, a sensational speaker, a super sister, an extraordinary employee or

Reflection

How do you respond when everyone is looking for you?

• • •

How has God refreshed you during times of solitude with Him?

employer. We are virtuous women who are fearfully and wonderfully made (Psalm 139:14). We were born for such a time as this. That's why "Everyone is looking for you!"

Mark 1:32–39

[32] That evening after sunset the people brought to Jesus all the sick and demon-possessed. [33] The whole town gathered at the door, [34] and Jesus healed many who had various diseases. He also drove out many demons, but he would not let the demons speak because they knew who he was.

[35] Very early in the morning, while it was still dark, Jesus got up, left the house and went off to a solitary place, where he prayed. [36] Simon and his companions went to look for him, [37] and when they found him, they exclaimed: "Everyone is looking for you!"

[38] Jesus replied, "Let us go somewhere else—to the nearby villages—so I can preach there also. That is why I have come." [39] So he traveled throughout Galilee, preaching in their synagogues and driving out demons.

My Hiding Place

You are my hiding place;
you will protect me from trouble
and surround me with songs of deliverance.
I will instruct you and teach you
in the way you should go;
I will counsel you with my loving eye on you.

PSALM 32:7–8

Sometimes life becomes overwhelming. During my recovery from an overwhelming traumatic injury, God was my hiding place. The Lord covered me and watched over me in the midst of my trials, protecting me from further harm as I healed, rested, and recuperated.

The day-to-day troubles of this world can make us feel like we need to find a safe place to hide away to rest and recuperate. King David certainly felt this way, and he sought God as a hiding place in the midst of trouble (Psalm 17:8).

Imagine being a baby bird, shielded from danger under the shadow of the wings of a parent bird. Where we are weak, He is strong. God provides a hiding place, and He preserves us from trouble when we run to Him. We are safe in the shadow of His wings (Psalm 36:7).

When God delivered His children from trouble in biblical times, they often sang and danced to celebrate the great victories of God. We see this in the book of Exodus where God opened the path of dry ground in the middle of the sea to deliver His children out of slavery in Egypt. Moses sang a song of deliverance (Exodus 15:1–19). Then his sister Miriam led the women with a joyous dance as they sang and shook their tambourines to commemorate the great deliverance of the Lord (Exodus 15:20–21). To be surrounded by songs of deliverance implies great joy in the Lord's protection and preservation.

After we run to God for protection and preservation, and joyously celebrate Him for keeping us safe and delivering us from evil, He can instruct us and teach us the way that we should go (Psalm 32:8). He now has our full attention! The Scripture here says that God will "counsel us with [His] loving eye." That means He always has His eyes on us. Just like a mother looks at her child from afar to guide him in the way he or she should go just by a glance of her eye, God will direct us if we will keep our focus on Him.

> ### *Reflection*
>
> *Can you recall a time in your life when God was your hiding place?*
>
> • • •
>
> *How will you make a concentrated effort to allow God to direct you with His eye?*

Exodus 15:2–3

² The LORD is my strength and my defense;
   he has become my salvation.
He is my God, and I will praise him,
   my father's God, and I will exalt him.
³ The LORD is a warrior;
   the LORD is his name.

Breathe Love

Blessed be the Lord,
Who daily loads us with benefits,
The God of our salvation!
Selah

PSALM 68:19 (NKJV)

s I reflect on my time away in retreat, a smile graces my face. Selah—taking time to pause whether away or at home—gives me life! I'm a leader, manager, professor, motivator, sorority sister, mom, grand-mom, auntie, and daughter. The fixer, connector of people, and guardian of a toddler. Merely thinking about my roles can be exhausting and deflating.

Self-care is invigorating, not selfish or greedy. Special moments to laugh, cry, share our testimony, reconnect with old friends, and meet new ones, and find oneself breathes life into us. In fact, by taking care of ourselves, we can better serve those around us. The Bible indicates that it is proper—even necessary—to love oneself to a reasonable degree. Such love includes caring for, respecting, and having a sense of self-worth (see Matthew 10:31).

Rather than glorifying selfishness, the Bible puts self-love in its rightful place. The second greatest commandment is this: "Love your neighbor as yourself" (Mark 12:31; Leviticus 19:18). Steps to self-care include sleeping the appropriate number of hours each night, clean eating, exercising three to five times a week, repeating positive affirmations to combat negative thoughts, thoughtfully engaging in meditation, journaling, forgiving yourself, saying no, and connecting positively with others.

Flight attendants' routine instructions can guide us on self-care: "Put your oxygen mask on first." Care for yourself before helping another. We simply cannot care for others unless we make ourselves a priority. Once we do so—once we breathe in some self-love—we can then help those around us.

> *Reflection*
>
> How does understanding your value from God's view help you reconsider self-care?

In our busy culture, oftentimes we are running without oxygen, empty, thinking, *If I do just a little more—check more tasks off my list, work just a little harder, help more family and friends—it will all be OK. I'm strong. I can keep going.* Sure, we can, until we pass out, get sick, or succumb to injury, which often is our body's reaction to our efforts to be superhuman. It is the Spirit's reminder that our power comes not from seeing how much more we can cram into a day, but from truly appreciating the day we have, the life we have, and those who are in it. That is where real power can be felt and seen.

I agree with God: to love myself and to make myself a priority. I will press pause and take a selah because my family is worth it. My team is worth it. My community is worth it. I am worth it.

Matthew 10:29–31 (*KJV*)

[29] Are not two sparrows sold for a farthing? and one of them shall not fall on the ground without your Father.

[30] But the very hairs of your head are all numbered.

[31] Fear ye not therefore, ye are of more value than many sparrows.

Persevering Praise

Blessed is the one who perseveres
under trial because, having stood the test,
that person will receive the crown of life
that the Lord has promised to those who love him.

JAMES 1:12

*M*y greatest spiritual mentor, my mom, epitomized perseverance in the midst of tribulation. My most significant faith-shaping memory occurred when I was too young to fully understand it. Shortly after a fire destroyed our home, Mom kept on praising God. Leaning on Scripture for assurance, Mom knew the importance of putting praise into action. Because of her model, in part, I too have been able to praise God in the midst of trials.

Through trying times, I have come to find comfort in God's divine declarations and promises. One of my favorite assurances from Scripture says: "'For I know the plans I have for you,' declares the LORD, 'plans to prosper you and not to harm you, plans to give you hope and a future'" (Jeremiah 29:11). These beloved words have gotten me through many a struggle.

Not too long ago, back-to-back, life-altering events left me tattered. Praying the words of Jeremiah 29:11 gave me solace. While I was praying the verses, though, I realized my spirit wasn't *praising*. Although I was repeating those powerful words, I was still depleted, frustrated, and isolated. Then, by God's providence, the invitation to a special retreat arrived. I was reluctant to attend because I had my own biased assumptions about such a retreat. (These concerns would actually be addressed and alleviated throughout the retreat.) From booking travel to arriving at the retreat, I experienced a whirlwind of conflicting emotions, from reluctance to anticipation.

In the first retreat session, we briefly introduced ourselves. Although I don't remember what I said, I do recall crying throughout my introduction. My heart was racing. Later, my extroverted roommate kindly shared her testimony. Subsequently, throughout the days, I would meditate on the retreat's prayer and theme, which was *selah*: pause, reflect, and listen to God! Everything—from guest speaker presentations and testimonies, fitness breaks, prayer times, and meditation sessions—aligned with that agenda, and I experienced a breakthrough. I began to praise God.

The result of the retreat for me was revelation, release, and rejuvenation. I heard: *trust must be put into action.* Our sharing in this retreat space of selah had impact, confirming the necessity of praise even during the storms in our lives. I found that other women's stories were my stories too. Here were a few of my takeaways:

- When there is an absence of trust in God, there is a potential for anxiety that hinders hope and endurance.

- One objective of trials is to alter—not tatter—and re-focus us to create a balance between self-reliance and spiritual reliance. The apostle Paul, Martin Luther King Jr., Mother Teresa, Mandela, and others' life experiences bear this out.

- We are spiritual beings going through human experiences—life's struggles—according to God's purpose for our lives. Assurances, like Jeremiah 29:11, are fortified when *actions* of trust in the form of praise prevail in us throughout our tests. The action of praise is a freewill offering, a blessing to us that stirs the strength of the Almighty.

> **Reflection**
>
> *How do you put trust into action when you are going through trials?*
>
> • • •
>
> *How's your praise?*

If in doubt—*selah*—immerse yourself into the Scriptures and spend time with God until you are delivered. Believe and praise in spite of your circumstances!

James 1:2–8 (NKJV)

[2] My brethren, count it all joy when you fall into various trials, [3] knowing that the testing of your faith produces patience. [4] But let patience have its perfect work, that you may be perfect and complete, lacking nothing. [5] If any of you lacks wisdom, let him

ask of God, who gives to all liberally and without reproach, and it will be given to him. ⁶ But let him ask in faith, with no doubting, for he who doubts is like a wave of the sea driven and tossed by the wind. ⁷ For let not that man suppose that he will receive anything from the Lord; ⁸ he is a double-minded man, unstable in all his ways.

God be merciful to us

and bless us,

And cause His face

to shine upon us.

Selah

PSALM 67:1 (NKJV)

Seasons in God's Light

*O*ne of the joys of going away to college was discovering ways to let my personality shine in my place and space. I had a little, old dorm room, but I could dress it up and make it my own. No one else had to like it or to approve it. It was mine. My expression—taste, colors. My personality. In college, you knew whose room you were in by its *touch* and various accents. My junior year in Boston at Emerson College, I lived in a beautiful brownstone in the Back Bay. One year, we female students had "a thing" with fishnets. We asked our male friends to help us secure them in all kinds of creative patterns with hooks and tacks on the ceilings and walls, and on our bed frames. My favorite colors were purple and gold, the colors of our school, so I had a gold fishnet, and then purple bed linens. I put my personal touch all over the room and hung posters of Angela Davis, Martin Luther King Jr., and Sly and the Family Stone. And the music that moved me—Minnie Riperton's "Lovin' You"—played all day, every day. People knew when they entered my room, they were coming into *my* place.

Likewise, when one comes into *God's place* on retreat, God has set the atmosphere. God often offers brilliant sunrises to start our days, beautiful skies, and calming seas. He loves us enough to allow us to start the day, too, and He shares life with us. As the old folks used to say, "There are some that didn't rise to see this brand-new day."

I've absorbed the majestic artistry of our Savior on seaside retreats and believe there's nothing more beautiful, more awesome than meeting God at God's place. Seeing the beauty in the sky with its pastel, paintbrush-like strokes is certainly a wonderful way to begin and end any day. At night, there's moonlight shining, and it seems God has turned the lights on for me. I love it when God speaks to me through the sunrise and the moon's glow. It's very personal, just me and God. And no two days are alike. It's an honor and privilege to enter God's presence, where He has set the atmosphere and "decorated" the place with His special touches.

Sometimes on retreat by the ocean, I have tried to capture the scenes on my cell phone camera. But by the end of the week, I've learned to capture the beauty in my heart and soul and enjoy simply being in God's presence with no technology, with deep appreciation for the natural and supernatural experience in Him. Selah makes a space for memories that don't need to be recorded. The memories remain, reminding us at a later date that we need to pause rather than be *on*: to relax in the "beauty of [His] holiness" (Psalm 96:9 KJV). This feels awesome. Selah allows us to go from so much structure to regaining our spiritual stride. It's a season of rest, rejuvenation, and reflection.

In pausing for time with God, there's nothing between "me and Thee," as they say. In retreat, I lean into God's light. His gifts of sunrises and sunsets, and the light of His presence. In whatever season you're in and no matter the struggles you face, I invite you to enter into—soak in—God's light.

When each one of us stops long enough, we can notice and hear God. Carving out time for God within our own space and schedule, we retreat and hide in the presence of our Savior, to enjoy and savor His goodness and love for us. It's a beautiful time. It's a great season that can carry us throughout other seasons of life.

—Suzan D. Johnson Cook

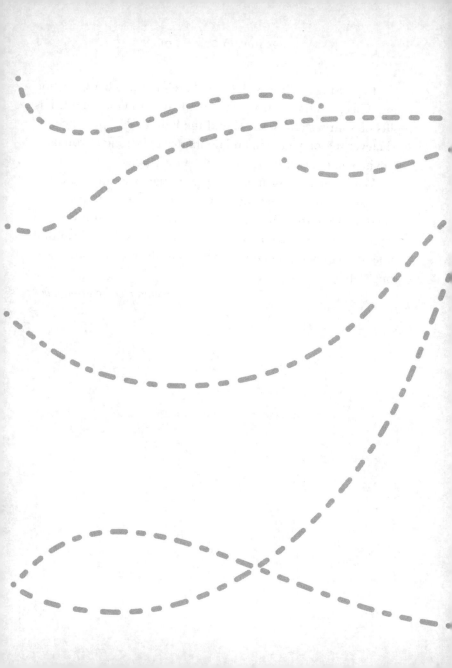

Embracing Our Seasons

There is a time for everything,
and a season for every activity under the heavens.

ECCLESIASTES 3:1

I grew up in Jamaica until I was a junior in high school. Due to the tropical climate, there was no real variation in the seasons. At best, there were two seasons: a rainy season and dry season, but the temperatures were constant. I did not experience the four seasons until I relocated to New York. I moved in the summer, so there wasn't much difference in the weather initially. However, I soon witnessed summer turn to fall with its gilded glow and gorgeous colors. Then, winter took sway with its drab gray skies and abridged daylight. Just when I thought I wouldn't survive another dreary winter day, spring made her grand entrance with birds singing and the leaves and flowers waking up from their long nap. Boom! Just like that, I experienced the beauty and the blemishes of all four seasons, and I took it all in with wide-eyed wonder.

Even after living in North America for decades, I am still fascinated by the seasons. The most important lesson that I have learned from the shifting of the seasons is that change is consistent and constant. Every season in our lives is temporary, and it is up to us to decipher the value in each. As much as we would like our lives to be filled with only rainbows and roses, the reality is that we will also have what one songwriter has preserved as "seasons of distress and grief." Nobody likes pain, disappointment, or any sense of discomfort. Our instinct during the down and difficult seasons is to figure how to get out as quickly as possible. Ecclesiastes 3:1–8 reminds us that there is a season for everything under the sun. The timing is not up to us, so we have to embrace each season and ride it out.

For example, in 2017, Hurricane Harvey pummeled Houston with rain for six days, but it felt like sixty days. It seemed we were going to be forever cooped up inside, and our lives would turn to mildew. In the end, it was still temporary, because no storm lasts forever. We also have to make sure we figure out the lesson or the blessing from each season. Someday we will be able to share our testimony with someone struggling with the same experience, and be a blessing to them.

Women of a certain age often joke about *personal summers* (hot flashes). The reality is, though, that every individual's seasons are personal. For this reason, let us not waste time or energy comparing someone else's seasons to ours. When we see another sister in her winning season, let us simply cele-

Reflection

*Ask yourself,
What are the
biggest challenges
I face when transitioning between the
different seasons
of my life, and what
has been the most
effective strategy
for managing them?*

brate her and jump for joy for her, just as Miss Nigeria did for her fellow competitor Miss Jamaica when Miss Jamaica won the title at the Miss World 2019 pageant! The truth is we have no idea what a sister has lost during a "losing season." When she's in her season of loss, let us endeavor to be a source of encouragement and comfort. And when we are in our winning season, let us be mindful that it is temporary. Let us be present to its unique gifts. May it be a reminder that no matter how many dark days we endure, the sun will shine again.

Ecclesiastes 3:1–8

¹ There is a time for everything,
>   and a season for every activity under the heavens:

>   ² a time to be born and a time to die,
>   a time to plant and a time to uproot,
>   ³ a time to kill and a time to heal,
>   a time to tear down and a time to build,
>   ⁴ a time to weep and a time to laugh,
>   a time to mourn and a time to dance,
>   ⁵ a time to scatter stones and a time to gather them,
>   a time to embrace and a time to refrain from embracing,
>   ⁶ a time to search and a time to give up,
>   a time to keep and a time to throw away,
>   ⁷ a time to tear and a time to mend,
>   a time to be silent and a time to speak,
>   ⁸ a time to love and a time to hate,
>   a time for war and a time for peace.

Great Expectations

Suddenly, their eyes were opened,
and they recognized him.
And at that moment he disappeared!

LUKE 24:31 (NLT)

*W*hen my children were younger, one of their favorite games was hide-and-seek. The funny thing about the two youngest, Natalie and Johnny, is that they often hid in clever places. One time, a big basket full of freshly laundered clothes caught Johnny's eye. He jumped inside the pile and managed to stay hidden and still. "Ready or not, here I come!" shouted Natalie. She scampered to all of Johnny's usual hiding places. But no Johnny. She called for him, but he didn't answer. In desperation, Natalie eventually plopped down by the big basket and began crying. "I'll never find him!" she started to scream, thinking her search was fruitless. Then Johnny popped up, exclaiming, "Here I am, Natalie! Don't cry!" Then they hugged and ran off to play. Aren't there times when God does not show up in the way we expect and we respond in frustration, *Where are you?*

When Jesus didn't show up in a way His followers could comprehend, the people closest to Jesus believed their hopes and great expectations about Him had been dashed. The third day after Jesus's crucifixion, two of His disciples confided in each other about their bewilderment over His seeming absence (Luke 24). Though Jesus had warned His disciples to expect that He would be crucified and resurrected in three days, these followers were also grappling with the report that Jesus's body was missing from the burial tomb (vv. 23–24). They were perplexed. God had hidden His identity so when Jesus appeared, engaging them in conversation—they couldn't recognize Him (vv. 15–16).

We may think God does not hear our cries, or He can't see our pain, or He is silent. We enter challenging seasons of life, observing circumstances we simply don't understand and even dilemmas we may deem too difficult for God to change. But God is with us, even when He appears to be hidden, and His plans for us are unfinished.

Jesus had to remind His troubled followers, "'You find it so hard to believe all that the prophets wrote in the Scriptures. Wasn't it clearly predicted that the Messiah would have to suffer all these things before entering his glory?' Then Jesus took them through the writings of Moses and all the prophets, explaining from all the Scriptures the things concerning himself" (vv. 25–27). Jesus reminded the disciples walking on the road to Emmaus not only what He said would surely happen but what all of Scripture had said about Him.

As we navigate life, we can focus on the Word of God: all of God's promises. When things do not go as anticipated, it may be easier to eye our unmet expectations rather than remember what He has taught us. However, the Holy Spirit guides us to keep our eyes on God and focus on His light, considering what He has done and has promised to do. The disciples persuaded Jesus to stay with them and have supper, and as they spent time together with Him, they noticed how Jesus took bread, blessed it, and gave it to them. They began to see that Jesus was alive! They saw what was familiar in the unfamiliar.

Focusing on Jesus, we can see God at work in the ordinary, and in the unfamiliar. When we stay in His Word, even during the gaps and pauses of life, it's a sweet surrender to His will and His ways. In these pauses, He will draw us nearer to himself, so we can experience more of His light.

Luke 24:19–34 (NLT)

19 "What things?" Jesus asked.

"The things that happened to Jesus, the man from Nazareth," they said. "He was a prophet who did powerful miracles, and he was a mighty teacher in the eyes of God and all the people. 20 But our leading priests and other religious leaders handed him over to be condemned to death, and they crucified him. 21 We had hoped he was the Messiah who had come to rescue Israel. This all happened three days ago.

Reflection

In what areas are you experiencing the unfamiliar?

• • •

What are you expecting from God?

• • •

How can you surrender your expectations in exchange for a closer walk with our gracious heavenly Father?

[22] "Then some women from our group of his followers were at his tomb early this morning, and they came back with an amazing report. [23] They said his body was missing, and they had seen angels who told them Jesus is alive! [24] Some of our men ran out to see, and sure enough, his body was gone, just as the women had said."

[25] Then Jesus said to them, "You foolish people! You find it so hard to believe all that the prophets wrote in the Scriptures. [26] Wasn't it clearly predicted that the Messiah would have to suffer all these things before entering his glory?" [27] Then Jesus took them through the writings of Moses and all the prophets, explaining from all the Scriptures the things concerning himself.

[28] By this time they were nearing Emmaus and the end of their journey. Jesus acted as if he were going on, [29] but they begged him, "Stay the night with us, since it is getting late." So he went home with them. [30] As they sat down to eat, he took the bread and blessed it. Then he broke it and gave it to them. [31] Suddenly, their eyes were opened, and they recognized him. And at that moment he disappeared!

[32] They said to each other, "Didn't our hearts burn within us as he talked with us on the road and explained the Scriptures to us?" [33] And within the hour they were on their way back to Jerusalem. There they found the eleven disciples and the others who had gathered with them, [34] who said, "The Lord has really risen! He appeared to Peter."

Letting Go to Listen

Be still, and know that I am God.

PSALM 46:10

We move through a time of change as we prepare for winter and let go of summer. In many landscapes, the autumn season causes the trees to boast beautiful, bold hues. As many trees shed their leaves, light rain makes way for blue skies, big white clouds, and rainbows. What a great time to stop, transition, and let go of fear and complacency.

Though the days leading up to my autumn retreat were filled with turmoil—a cousin dying in hospice, job pressures and burnout from traveling overseas, and doubt that I was fulfilling my life purpose—this verse reminded me God truly is in control: "Be still, and know that I am God; I will be exalted among the nations, I will be exalted in the earth" (Psalm 46:10). This resonated in my soul.

The weekend retreat was a pivotal moment for me. Entering the retreat space, I thought of the many roles I had taken on—with family, friends, community, and work. I knew my life had been out of balance.

God invited me to step away from the craziness of work, home, and world events to pause and reflect on the strengths

He had given me to share. Welcoming the beautiful rest, I opened my heart to hear God's messages in that sacred time.

My life purpose is to mentor and invest in the life journeys of young people and professionals. Sometimes, though, I serve and nurture others at a cost to my own well-being. While pouring into others when they need me, I am prone to feel selfish when taking time for myself. At the retreat, I realized I was depleted: physically, mentally, and spiritually.

That weekend, I was at a breaking point, but God sent women to empower, embrace, and nurture me. I lacked the preparation for letting go and being present in the moment. But by the time I departed, I claimed my place. I accepted, *I'm in the right place, at the right time, for the right reasons. I need to retreat for me.*

When remaining still and allowing God to speak to us, there are boundless opportunities to be blessed. Stillness helps quiet our voice, so we can hear God's. I experienced God's presence in that place, both as I listened to Him in prayer and when I worshiped with my sisters. There, I could relinquish my need to be in control. In that season of change and transition, I realized the importance of pausing, breathing, and practicing self-care to honor my relationship with God.

Reflection

In this time of selah, how will you let go and listen to God's voice?

Selah gives us the moments we need to rest and consider God and listen to the magnificent truths He wants to tell us. Including His wonderful work in us.

Psalm 1

¹ Blessed is the one
   who does not walk in step with the wicked
or stand in the way that sinners take
   or sit in the company of mockers,
² but whose delight is in the law of the LORD,
   and who meditates on his law day and night.
³ That person is like a tree planted by streams of water,
   which yields its fruit in season
and whose leaf does not wither—
   whatever they do prospers.

⁴ Not so the wicked!
   They are like chaff
   that the wind blows away.
⁵ Therefore the wicked will not stand in the judgment,
   nor sinners in the assembly of the righteous.

⁶ For the LORD watches over the way of the righteous,
   but the way of the wicked leads to destruction.

When It Doesn't Happen

The LORD himself will fight for you. Just stay calm.

EXODUS 14:14 (NLT)

*J**ust make it happen.* These words drove my work as a corporate marketing maven for years. Education and experience taught me to always have a contingency plan—sometimes several. A well-executed plan A usually did the job, but if not, plan B would pick up the slack. Plan C's purpose was to mend any breach in the previous two. Plan D waited in the wings to resuscitate failing plans but was seldom necessary. Success on some level was assured.

But have you ever been in a season when *making it happen* does not equal a slam dunk? Whether it's starting a business or a new career, pursuing personal or financial elevation, parenting, or managing a health crisis—what happens when you've done your best, but your back is still against the wall? What happens when, in the pursuit of accomplishing your goals, all your contingencies crumble?

What happens when you find yourself trapped, separated or isolated in a space that prevents moving to success? When you've implemented all of your plans, while maintaining your composure, values, and beliefs, and the results are slim? When your emotions beckon a trip down a darker path toward victory, by any means necessary? When your will to *make it happen* stalls? When you realize that you cannot move any further in your own strength because your talents and abilities don't seem to be enough? This is when your confidence gives way to self-doubt, and faith meets fear.

When I think about Moses leading the Israelites out of captivity in Egypt, I am reminded of the Israelites' fear and Moses's faith. Moses *spoke*, cried out to the Lord. Moses *listened* to the Lord for instructions that he couldn't visualize. Moses *obeyed* the Lord, no matter how outlandish God's plan A might have seemed. Three things are worth noting for those of us who've tried—and failed— at *just making it happen*. First, the Israelites' were emotionally defeated, and it showed in their behavior, as they felt trapped on all sides. When you're in tough circumstances, monitor your attitudes and behaviors even more closely. Guard against submitting to defeat, as the Israelites did. Second, in spite of their complaints, God allowed the cloud of light and fire to guide the grumbling Israelites and to protect them from the Egyptian army. Remember, God is with you—regardless of what you see or feel. And third, only God had the power to *make it*

Reflection

What are you
believing God for?
How are you
releasing your plans
to His power?

• • •

How is your
attitude different
from the Israelites?

happen—a miraculous escape route through the middle of the Red Sea. As much as you might trust your talents and abilities, remember, in the end, it's the power of God that brings about miracles.

Because of Moses's faith connection, God used him to deliver His promise to the Israelites: that they would possess the land of the Canaanites, Hittites, Amorites, Hivites, and Jebusites (Exodus 13:5)! And God was glorified.

In retrospect, now I understand that trying to make things happen in my own power pales in comparison to the power of the Holy Spirit that lives inside me. Life is teaching me that my faith connection with God is always the ultimate game changer! No one ever said there wouldn't be times of trial and seasons of tribulations. But, regardless of the turmoil that surrounds me—be it a wall of water on the right and on the left, God's power is ever-present in every season and circumstance. His protection lights my path and His purpose for my life will be accomplished.

If God can execute a radical move like parting the Red Sea for the Israelites, He can certainly see us through our storms and calm our seas.

Exodus 14:1–14

¹ Then the LORD said to Moses, ² "Tell the Israelites to turn back and encamp near Pi Hahiroth, between Migdol and the sea. They are to encamp by the sea, directly opposite Baal Zephon. ³ Pharaoh will think, 'The Israelites are wandering around the land in confusion, hemmed in by the desert.' ⁴ And I will harden Pharaoh's heart, and he will pursue them. But I

will gain glory for myself through Pharaoh and all his army, and the Egyptians will know that I am the LORD." So the Israelites did this.

⁵ When the king of Egypt was told that the people had fled, Pharaoh and his officials changed their minds about them and said, "What have we done? We have let the Israelites go and have lost their services!" ⁶ So he had his chariot made ready and took his army with him. ⁷ He took six hundred of the best chariots, along with all the other chariots of Egypt, with officers over all of them. ⁸ The LORD hardened the heart of Pharaoh king of Egypt, so that he pursued the Israelites, who were marching out boldly. ⁹ The Egyptians—all Pharaoh's horses and chariots, horsemen and troops—pursued the Israelites and overtook them as they camped by the sea near Pi Hahiroth, opposite Baal Zephon.

¹⁰ As Pharaoh approached, the Israelites looked up, and there were the Egyptians, marching after them. They were terrified and cried out to the LORD. ¹¹ They said to Moses, "Was it because there were no graves in Egypt that you brought us to the desert to die? What have you done to us by bringing us out of Egypt? ¹² Didn't we say to you in Egypt, 'Leave us alone; let us serve the Egyptians'? It would have been better for us to serve the Egyptians than to die in the desert!"

¹³ Moses answered the people, "Do not be afraid. Stand firm and you will see the deliverance the LORD will bring you today. The Egyptians you see today you will never see again. ¹⁴ The LORD will fight for you; you need only to be still."

• ——— *Marcia A. Harris* ——— •

See Those Swings?

Trust in Him at all times, you people;
Pour out your heart before Him;
God is a refuge for us.   *Selah*

PSALM 62:8 (NASB)

om, Aunt Val, watch this!" was the cry from my nine-year-old daughter, Lesley. We were at the park for an interchurch softball game. It was the ninth inning. The score was three against our two runs. The bases were loaded, and two players had struck out. Lesley was at bat. She set up at the plate and awaited the pitch. When the pitcher threw, Lesley swung with all her nine-year-old might. She missed.

"Strike one!" the umpire yelled.

Lesley stepped out of the batter's box and looked up into the stands at us as we all stood there shouting: "Come on, Lesley! You can do it; you can do it; you can do it!"

She stepped back into position. Set up her bat. Looked up at us and then at the pitcher. Again came the pitch, Lesley's swing, and the miss.

"Strike two!" the umpire yelled.

With disappointment, Lesley hung her head and stepped

out of the batter's box again. We all screamed at her: "Come on, Lesley! You can do it! You can do it! You can do it!" She stepped back in. Lesley gave the biggest swing she had in her. That was strike three. She was out—leaving three players stranded on the bases. The game was over. We had lost. As we emptied the stands, I ran over to Lesley and hugged her. She turned her big eyes up to me and looked into mine. "It's OK, sweetheart; you tried your best. You gave it all you had," I said as I tousled her hair.

She sighed. Then she looked up at me again and said with excitement, "Mom! Mom, were you watching! Did you see those swings? Can you imagine if one of them had connected? It would have been a home run!" Tears streamed down my face as I held her close. Lesley is an adult now, but the lesson she demonstrated that day lives on. It's not that we are always going to win in life. What counts is that we give life all that we have and not become discouraged. We must give our best shot and leave the rest up to Him. Connecting is His part—not ours.

Reflection

How has God revealed His presence to you?

• • •

How has your confidence in Him comforted you when you've missed the mark or lost in your life pursuits?

• • •

What do you need God to help you achieve, and do you have His peace about it?

The prophet Isaiah shares with us a promise in his writings that gives us encouragement to face the upheavals of life with strength and courage. We are told that He gives strength to the weary and increases the power of the weak (Isaiah 40:29). With God's ordained strength, we can take our best swings at life and even when we might feel defeated, our Lord offers us solace and meets us in our shortcomings. We can count on His strength, and He promised to give us peace (Philippians 4:9).

So, go ahead. Step up to that plate. Take your best swing at life. God is watching, and He is with you!

Philippians 4:4–9

[4] Rejoice in the Lord always. I will say it again: Rejoice! [5] Let your gentleness be evident to all. The Lord is near. [6] Do not be anxious about anything, but in every situation, by prayer and petition, with thanksgiving, present your requests to God. [7] And the peace of God, which transcends all understanding, will guard your hearts and your minds in Christ Jesus.

[8] Finally, brothers and sisters, whatever is true, whatever is noble, whatever is right, whatever is pure, whatever is lovely, whatever is admirable—if anything is excellent or praise-worthy—think about such things. [9] Whatever you have learned or received or heard from me, or seen in me—put it into practice. And the God of peace will be with you.

Trust in Him at all times,

you people;

Pour out your hearts before Him;

God is a refuge for us.

Selah

PSALM 62:8 (NASB)

Being Still

I've learned God can speak to and through us in any way He wants—through people, in the stillness of our solitary quiet times, and often through nature. Waves dance and speak to me through their divine choreography, along with trees that sway, swarms of birds and butterflies that flit and alight, the rising and setting of the sun, and seeing the different stages of the moon. As He suspends the elements in the sky, we just see stillness, not their motion. Stillness is necessary for us too. For me, being in nature quiets my soul. Stillness is necessary for all of us. Sitting still, *being* still so that the creation—that's us—reconnects and focuses our hearts on our Creator. We can stand still even when life challenges us to react in fight-or-flight mode. We can draw nearer to listen, see, and simply be in the presence of God, while admiring all His handiwork.

We are in the midst of so much busyness. It is necessary to mandate—command—our souls to be still. *Soul, do you hear me: be still and listen—hear an unspoken, inaudible language— as the Holy Spirit connects us to God.* Like Aretha's song says, "sacred scenes [will] unfold."

Now I see why even the winds and the waves obey God's will. In selah moments, He reminds us to be at peace, because the Almighty is with us always, even to the end (Matthew 28:20).

In my pause, my selah, by witnessing God's creation I was driven back to the book of Genesis, where He began all this creating. Sometimes in life, we're so busy moving that we miss going back to the Word of God. So, while on my selah sabbatical, I revisit the Sabbath, and I keep time for God holy. The day of the week we call Sabbath is not as important as setting aside time with God. And the true work of the Sabbath involves loving Him and our neighbor, therefore, doing justice—becoming the fabric of our being.

As a senior pastor, I was always working on Sundays, leading worship, counseling, preaching, and teaching, so that others in the congregation could partake of and participate with God. So, I always reserved Mondays as my Sabbath time with God. That was my time when I was not "working worship," but rather simply worshiping in the "beauty of His holiness" (1 Chronicles 16:29 NKJV).

In his book *The Genesee Diary*, Henri Nouwen wrote about how he, a priest, checked himself into a monastery for a silent retreat. He recalls that he had been so busy talking about prayer that he had lost his *actual* prayer time. He had been so busy giving speeches and talks about God that He had stopped talking *with* God. Sabbath is so important. His "still small voice" speaks (1 Kings 19:12 KJV). In my silent moments, *I* can hear God. It wasn't that God hadn't been speaking all along. Perhaps, just perhaps, I had been moving too fast, with far too much on my plate to truly listen.

In Isaiah 6:8, God asks the prophet Isaiah a couple of questions: "Whom shall I send?" and "Who will go for us?"

Finally, Isaiah answers, "Here am I; send me" (KJV). All along, as shown earlier in chapter 6, God had been trying to get Isaiah's attention. King Uzziah, the king for whom Isaiah worked, had just died (v. 1). God had removed Isaiah from his busyness with King Uzziah, who had been the focus of Isaiah's gaze. Only then did Isaiah see and hear God, exclaiming, "Mine eyes have seen the King, the LORD of hosts" (Isaiah 6:5 KJV).

I definitely identify with Isaiah because he worked as a senior-level executive in the king's court. He held a position as chief of staff. Like one who works in the West Wing of the White House, in that prominent position you have a lot of privileges and perks. You are invited to events and social gatherings that the average person cannot attend. So, if you're not careful—and I dare say *prayerful*—there can be a loss of perspective. If you attend enough of these events with the president by your side (or in Isaiah's case, the king—the ruler) you can begin to think you have authority and privileges you really don't have. You might think you don't need anyone else. How many times have we heard folks say, "I'm a self-made woman," or "I'm a self-made man"?

When King Uzziah was gone from the scene, Isaiah's gaze was on God, who caused Isaiah to reprioritize. That's what pausing and stillness will do: allow you to hear the truest Voice and see the King of Kings.

God still speaks. May we take time to be still and get to know Him. He is the One who allows us to stand—even before kings and presidents.

—*Suzan D. Johnson Cook*

Still Strong

Your eyes saw my unformed body;
all the days ordained for me were written in your book
before one of them came to be.

PSALM 139:16

There are some one hundred and fifty women listed in the Bible. Some are named, others anonymous. If I were to interview them, I don't think many of these sisters ever had an inkling their testimonies would stay strong for generations, and be read by millions throughout the world. Today, anyone who has come in contact with an organized religious group knows about Mary, the mother of Jesus, maybe Jezebel from the Old Testament, and so many others. God has placed these biblical women on the world stage for us to learn from their lives, their stories.

Some of the women in the Bible have common household names. But then there are the not-so-obvious women, like Rizpah. The first time I heard her name, I asked, *Who is this woman, and what did she do?* And I found out her biblical testimony: she dared to ask King David to give her children a proper burial. She had kept wild animals away from her sons' and their male cousins' bodies after they had been hung on a hillside at David's command. David had agreed to the killings to avenge a tribe named the Gibeonites (2 Samuel 21:1–14). For a long time, I wondered why her story had been recorded: what are we to learn from such an unusual situation? And, why would God place her on the world stage? Until I considered her strength to still stand in the face of such pain.

The variety of women God placed in Scripture has always fascinated me, from pure virgins to persecuted prostitutes. It lets me know that "God does not show favoritism" (Acts 10:34). Could I find myself lining up behind biblical women and teaching a simple or profound message with my life—in front of a worldwide audience, as they did? That's a scary thought. It's also humbling. The question makes me want to scramble, quickly clean up my life—at least straighten up my habits. But when I examine and reflect on Psalm 139:16, I relax in God's arms. The psalmist wrote, "All the days ordained for me were written in your book before one of them came to be."

God has a book of our life's story: He knows how our lives started, how they're going to end, every detail in the middle (Psalm 90:1–3). But we don't. Neither did the people in Scripture. As we see in many stories, God took them by surprise. A raggedy page from their

Reflection

What about your life do you want to take to God rather than attempt to clean up or fix on your own?

* * *

How might your pain and mistakes serve as a part of your testimony?

life story God smoothed out and placed in the notebook of His story.

Lord, You have our book in Your hands: our stories and how You want us to tell them. Stories already written. We are standing in You, Lord, confident. You will perform it all. As we pause to commune with You, help us rest in Your plan.

Psalm 90

¹ LORD, you have been our dwelling place
    throughout all generations.
² Before the mountains were born
    or you brought forth the whole world,
    from everlasting to everlasting you are God.

³ You turn people back to dust,
    saying, "Return to dust, you mortals."
⁴ A thousand years in your sight
    are like a day that has just gone by,
    or like a watch in the night.
⁵ Yet you sweep people away in the sleep of death—
    they are like the new grass of the morning:
⁶ In the morning it springs up new,
    but by evening it is dry and withered.

⁷ We are consumed by your anger
    and terrified by your indignation.
⁸ You have set our iniquities before you,
    our secret sins in the light of your presence.

⁹ All our days pass away under your wrath;
    we finish our years with a moan.
¹⁰ Our days may come to seventy years,
    or eighty, if our strength endures;
yet the best of them are but trouble and sorrow,
    for they quickly pass, and we fly away.
¹¹ If only we knew the power of your anger!
    Your wrath is as great as the fear that is your due.
¹² Teach us to number our days,
    that we may gain a heart of wisdom.

¹³ Relent, LORD! How long will it be?
    Have compassion on your servants.
¹⁴ Satisfy us in the morning with your unfailing love,
    that we may sing for joy and be glad all our days.
¹⁵ Make us glad for as many days as you have afflicted us,
    for as many years as we have seen trouble.
¹⁶ May your deeds be shown to your servants,
    your splendor to their children.

¹⁷ May the favor of the LORD our God rest on us;
    establish the work of our hands for us—
    yes, establish the work of our hands.

Are You Listening?

This is what the Lord says:
"A voice is heard in Ramah,
mourning and great weeping,
Rachel weeping for her children
and refusing to be comforted,
because they are no more."

JEREMIAH 31:15

ecently, as I rode the Metro in the Washington, DC, area, my route crossed the Potomac River. I was reminded that my enslaved ancestors had crossed the same river hundreds of years before in the early seventeenth century. I remembered the sacrifices of my ancestors, the power of God's grace, and the emancipation legislation of 1863 and 1865 that makes it possible for Pan-African peoples to travel today. Without these gifts, I know I would not be living an emancipated life, or living out my calling in Jesus Christ as a fully free person. I rejoice in these gifts while also being held accountable to care for those oppressed by unjust systems of power. Here is my testimony from that day on the Metro.

On that day of travel, I thought I heard mourning and weeping not too far away from me. *Am I imagining this,* I thought, even as I listened to the haunting, piercing cries. *Am I envisioning my ancestors crossing the Potomac River?* I felt led to get up and follow what I realized were cries nearby. I made a startling discovery. A sister who sat in the middle of a crowd of travelers on the Metro train was the source of the great mourning and weeping.

I immediately felt led to go to her, pray with her, and share company with her. Then I felt led to invite her to share with me what was causing her to grieve in this public display. Through the eyes of faith, I saw my spiritual answer: she was a "Rachel," a woman in pain and struggle, whom God had promised to show His mercy (Jeremiah 31:15–16). As in the case of so many people, she had circumstances that led to such profound pain that she cried out her story: she and her family faced eviction that day, her mother was dying, and she was hungry.

Reflecting on this, I still don't know if I was more upset about the systemic issues of hunger and poverty that have contributed to her plight and to those of so many other "Rachels" today, or that her great mourning and weeping seemed to go unheard and undignified by other people's silence on the train that day.

Do we hear the deep mourning and weeping of God's wounded people today? I think many of us do hear and act honorably. Many of us do speak into others' pain. I give thanks to God for His promise to show mercy and love.

Jeremiah cautions and reminds us that there is a Rachel crying out in all of us for ourselves and for others. The prophet's message from God reminds us we are not alone. God is with us. May the words of Jeremiah be in us, work through us, and empower us to do all we can to love and to serve God and people. As we sit still in God's presence, may we learn anew how to love ourselves as our ancestors did before us, listening to and following our God.

Reflection

How is God responding to your cry for yourself, and for others?

Jeremiah 31:33–34

[33] "This is the covenant I will make with the people of
        Israel
    after that time," declares the LORD.
"I will put my law in their minds
    and write it on their hearts.
I will be their God,
    and they will be my people.
[34] No longer will they teach their neighbor,
    or say to one another, 'Know the LORD,'
because they will all know me,
    from the least of them to the greatest,"
        declares the LORD.
"For I will forgive their wickedness
    and will remember their sins no more."

When God Leads

> But Samuel replied:
> "Does the Lord delight in burnt offerings and sacrifices
> as much as in obeying the Lord?
> To obey is better than sacrifice,
> and to heed is better than the fat of rams."
>
> 1 SAMUEL 15:22

God spoke to my husband and me to leave a place where we had lived for twenty years, Kisumu, Kenya, to go to Nairobi. I must admit I resisted the move—for five years. Thinking my ministry work in Kisumu most valuable, I stalled and did not follow God's instructions. This reminds me of King Saul, anointed by God to lead Israel, who then did not fully follow God's instructions, to his ruin and the loss of his rule (see 1 Samuel 15). I avoided fulfilling the call to Nairobi—almost to my ruin.

In those five years, God allowed difficult circumstances. That changed my heart. Robbers attacked our home in Kisumu, stealing our money and other valuables at gunpoint. In another incident, in the aftermath of presidential elections, we experienced violence. As a woman leader in the Kisumu region, I was called to assist those dealing with trauma. I was nominated to attend a conference for leadership training.

At the training site, a violent group invaded the hotel, and I had to hide in a kitchen closet to avoid being attacked. Hours later, as I tried to go home, the group accosted me. I stared at death in my attackers' eyes. But God sent a lady who defended me as a mother of faith. That saved my life! After the hotel incident, I was fearful of walking or driving in the city.

Over a period of two years, I learned how to rest and regain my peace. I also attended a Selah retreat. Through time in retreat with other sisters, God's voice encouraged me to obey His leading.

God used difficult circumstances and situations together for our good and aligned us with His will. God assured my husband and me that our time in Kisumu was up! When we obeyed God and moved to Nairobi, God orchestrated that the people who sold us our new estate (whom we had never met) would donate all their furniture and kitchen utensils for our new house.

Scripture says that God opens doors no man (or woman) can open and that He closes doors that no one else can (Revelation 3:7). He brings beginnings, creates new days in our lives, and establishes new purposes and paths. Each day, He is faithful, and has taught me to obey His voice and be led by His Spirit.

Reflection

What path or new beginning do you sense God has for you in your life and ministry? How can you lean in to God's choice for your life despite fear?

Revelation 3:7–13

⁷ To the angel of the church in Philadelphia write:

These are the words of him who is holy and true, who holds the key of David. What he opens no one can shut, and what he shuts no one can open. ⁸ I know your deeds. See, I have placed before you an open door that no one can shut. I know that you have little strength, yet you have kept my word and have not denied my name. ⁹ I will make those who are of the synagogue of Satan, who claim to be Jews though they are not, but are liars—I will make them come and fall down at your feet and acknowledge that I have loved you. ¹⁰ Since you have kept my command to endure patiently, I will also keep you from the hour of trial that is going to come on the whole world to test the inhabitants of the earth.

¹¹ I am coming soon. Hold on to what you have, so that no one will take your crown. ¹² The one who is victorious I will make a pillar in the temple of my God. Never again will they leave it. I will write on them the name of my God and the name of the city of my God, the new Jerusalem, which is coming down out of heaven from my God; and I will also write on them my new name. ¹³ Whoever has ears, let them hear what the Spirit says to the churches.

Standing Together

My soul glorifies the Lord
and my spirit rejoices in God my Savior,
for he has been mindful
of the humble state of his servant.

LUKE 1:46–48

I was desperate, broken, weary, and trying my best to fulfill God's purpose for my life. Drained emotionally from caring for my congregation and for all of the people from my village—those infected and affected by HIV and AIDS; abused women; pressing issues with children, and many other stresses and challenges—I knew I was on the verge of breaking down. I needed to be still and experience God's care. God gave me the space to stop: about that time, I was invited to a retreat about selah. I traveled almost two full days from South Africa to the United States to join my sisters in selah.

Scripture tells us how Mary went to visit her cousin Elizabeth after a visitation from the angel Gabriel, who told Mary news that was so confusing to her (Luke 1:26–39). Mary had committed herself to be "the Lord's servant," in Gabriel's presence (v. 38). But when Gabriel departed, Mary stopped everything to go and spend time with her cousin, whom the angel had confirmed was pregnant too. Elizabeth and her husband, Zechariah, had been unable to conceive until God's miraculous intervention, when she was very old (Luke 1:7). Scripture gives us the whole scene and includes their thoughts, heart, and soul.

> At that time Mary got ready and hurried to a town in the hill country of Judea, where she entered Zechariah's home and greeted Elizabeth. When Elizabeth heard Mary's greeting, the baby leaped in her womb, and Elizabeth was filled with the Holy Spirit. In a loud voice she exclaimed: "Blessed are you among women, and blessed is the child you will bear! . . . Blessed is she who has believed that the Lord would fulfill his promises to her!"
> (Luke 1:39–42, 45)

Elizabeth offered much-needed encouragement to Mary. When I finally came into the presence of my sisters in retreat, the whole community "shook" with love. All of the women stood for me! There were cries across the gathering. And I knew and felt our divine connection, at the place of rest God provided.

Several years later, after I lost my mother and my brother only two months apart, I became depressed and I could not grasp a way out of it. Through another invitation to a retreat, the Lord helped me to draw strength from Him. I was encouraged through the different speakers' messages and through the loving support of my sisters there. Again, I experienced selah moments: stopping, resting, reflecting, being restored, and relating. I was able to draw strength from God, including through different speakers' messages. Again, the Lord allowed me to return home, restored and full of hope.

In our desperate situations, our fellow Elizabeths can comfort us, strengthen us, and help us to press into our journey. Most of all, they can point us to the Lord, who knows our destiny.

I thank our Lord Jesus Christ who promises, "Come to me, all you who are weary and burdened, and I will give you rest" (Matthew 11:28). In all of our struggles, we can certainly go to God. Right where we are, and as we gather with others, when we can. Let's give our cares to Him. He will care for us, mind, body, and soul.

> **Reflection**
>
> *Where do you go to spend time with God and to find restoration with others?*

Luke 1:46–56

⁴⁶ And Mary said:

> "My soul glorifies the Lord
> ⁴⁷ and my spirit rejoices in God my Savior,
> ⁴⁸ for he has been mindful
> of the humble state of his servant.
> From now on all generations will call me blessed,
> ⁴⁹ for the Mighty One has done great things for me—
> holy is his name.

⁵⁰ His mercy extends to those who fear him,
    from generation to generation.
⁵¹ He has performed mighty deeds with his arm;
    he has scattered those who are proud in their inmost
        thoughts.
⁵² He has brought down rulers from their thrones
    but has lifted up the humble.
⁵³ He has filled the hungry with good things
    but has sent the rich away empty.
⁵⁴ He has helped his servant Israel,
    remembering to be merciful
⁵⁵ to Abraham and his descendants forever,
    just as he promised our ancestors."

⁵⁶ Mary stayed with Elizabeth for about three months and then returned home.

Sisters on the Seas

The earth is the LORD's, and everything in it,
the world, and all who live in it;
for he founded it on the seas
and established it on the waters.

PSALM 24:1–2

*A*s a Bahamian, I've been surrounded by water all my life, the beautiful turquoise waters of the Caribbean. The surroundings of my island have become even more beautiful as I have shared in retreat with my sisters there. As the psalmist writes, "The earth is the LORD's, and everything in it, the world, and all who live in it" (Psalm 24:1). I've seen the beauty of God's Earth and His people as I've been surrounded by the beauty of my sisters. Beautiful because we support one another in the Lord and stand in His strength together.

I was with Reverend Sujay as she began her ministry in Harlem, New York. I was new there, as I cared for my ailing aunt, and Sujay became my sister, and cared for me. She let me know that I was not alone in that big New York City. And every year since, she has invited me to the Selah retreat to be with sisters who love the Lord, and serve one another in love.

I've crossed the waters to meet with my sisters in Florida.

I hosted the sisters' retreat in Nassau, and one year we cruised from Florida to my hometown, where we had moments of selah not only on the ship, but as we disembarked. We worshiped together at the oldest Baptist church, Bethel Baptist Church. We enjoyed native foods together, we sang, we prayed, and we played together. Psalm 133, a song God's people shared as they worshiped together, says: "How good and pleasant it is when God's people live together in unity! It is like precious oil poured on the head, running down on the beard, running down on Aaron's beard, down on the collar of his robe. It is as if the dew of Hermon were falling on Mount Zion. For there the LORD bestows his blessing, even life forevermore."

Reflection

How have your own retreat experiences, alone and with other sisters, strengthened you?

There's something about selah moments that strengthen and help us. We sisters—tall, small, all shapes, all sizes—not only love experiencing retreat for ourselves but also for each other. We love simply being ourselves and gaining new strength. It's safe. It's fun. Laughter, leisure, spiritual care all wrapped up in one. Praise God.

Psalm 24

> [1] The earth is the LORD's, and everything in it,
>   the world, and all who live in it;
>   [2] for he founded it on the seas
>   and established it on the waters.

³ Who may ascend the mountain of the LORD?
   Who may stand in his holy place?
⁴ The one who has clean hands and a pure heart,
   who does not trust in an idol
   or swear by a false god.

⁵ They will receive blessing from the LORD
   and vindication from God their Savior.
⁶ Such is the generation of those who seek him,
   who seek your face, God of Jacob.

⁷ Lift up your heads, you gates;
   be lifted up, you ancient doors,
   that the King of glory may come in.
⁸ Who is this King of glory?
   The LORD strong and mighty,
   the LORD mighty in battle.
⁹ Lift up your heads, you gates;
   lift them up, you ancient doors,
   that the King of glory may come in.
¹⁰ Who is he, this King of glory?
   The LORD Almighty—
he is the King of glory.

I spread out my hands to You;

my soul longs for You

like a thirsty land.

Selah

PSALM 143:6 (NKJV)

Soul-Care Shifts

*S*oul-care practices help us to remain in sync with the Spirit in our hurried world. I'm from one of the largest and definitely one of the fastest cities in the world, New York, New York. So busy, they named it twice. The city is a secular one, so soul care is not prioritized in the main square or marketplace. So, one must be aware that her soul needs care.

I'm a woman who has birthed and raised children, a woman who was a daughter to ailing parents, a sister to an only sibling who died at age fifty-seven, and a senior pastor, trailblazing where there had been no path. Just saying all of this can wear one out. You can imagine the embodiment of all that is taxing physically, emotionally, mentally, and, sometimes, yes, spiritually. So just as we walk, swim, or work out to strengthen the body, I have had to find exercises for my soul. Just as we pause to eat solid food, I have had to learn to pause to take in *soul* food—spiritual nourishment—because I could not allow myself to try to do it all. If one doesn't strengthen the soul, you can fall. The writer Jude declares in that famous benediction:

"To him who is able to keep you from stumbling and to present you before his glorious presence without fault and with great joy—to the only God our Savior be glory, majesty, power and authority, through Jesus Christ our Lord, before all ages, now and forevermore! Amen" (Jude 24–25).

God will keep us from falling, and from *falling* apart! One of the ways I take in soul food is to memorize the Holy Scriptures, one at a time. When I'm reading and one speaks to me to the point where my soul flutters, I write it down in my journal. Then, I internalize it until it floods my soul, and my appetite for His Word is fed. What we eat in the natural affects our skin, nails, hair, teeth, and our brain. We need soul food that will be as nourishing to our soul as vitamins are to our physical body. Thinking on good things, digesting the Word with study, hearing the Word of God preached and preached well—all is soul food.

At retreat, we may also get dressed up, apply makeup, get a manicure, and go shopping together. But, more importantly, we learn more about how to "put on the whole armor of God" for the battles we left behind (Ephesians 6:11 NKJV). We find healing for the battle scars we carry on our souls, and courage for the battles we will face on the other side of our selah. For we are to "be strong in the Lord, and in the power of His might, [putting] on the whole armor of God" (Ephesians 6:10–11 NKJV).

When I can, I intentionally bask at the seashore for selah, on the sand in the sunshine, watching sunrises and sunsets. I sense the safe space with God and my sisters. If we can just make selah a key part of our lives, we can learn how to love the life we live and live the life we love. If we can hold on to God and stand still, we can go on a little while longer. By scheduling rest and reflection time on our calendars, we can escape becoming engulfed in the problems of the day-to-day personalities and responsibilities. The challenges don't disappear, but we can learn how to change our responses to them, learn new coping skills, and, especially, give and receive love from God (see page 204 for more tips).

At my seaside retreats, sisters flying in from all over the globe can take as long as two days to get to us, some making it in at bedtime. The women attending the retreat wait up for them. When a weary traveler walks through the door, the women applaud, cheer, and celebrate, so glad for their safe journey and arrival. They're often fatigued, exhausted, and yet they're exhilarated. Women can't *wait* to see their sisters, and to chill.

You can attend someone else's retreat, like mine, or organize one yourself—anytime and anywhere. It does not have to have a certain number of women, nor does it have to be large. I purposely began limiting our retreat number to forty, a biblical number, for intimacy, sharing, and caring. You know when *one* is missing from forty. If there are more than that, someone may get "lost in the crowd." You can always give yourself permission to have a selah all by yourself, with just you and God.

During retreat, we can find our prayin' power, playin' power, and stayin' power. We can leave our retreat renewed, re-energized, recharged, and restored. Try this formula for a successful selah:

- Vacate your regular schedule (even if you're staying home). Make time to invest in yourself spiritually and physically.

- Experience restoration. Try to rest and allow others to wait on you—and engage in fun and enjoyable leisure.

- Recreate. Allow that which you've poured out to be replenished by the Creator. Empty yourself from toxins with confession, fresh air, and relaxing time-outs. Allow yourself to be refilled and refueled.

—*Suzan D. Johnson Cook*

Rewarded

My grace is sufficient for you,
for my power is made perfect in weakness.

2 CORINTHIANS 12:9

or the first time in thirty years of ministry, God was not getting the glory out of my life, though I was attempting to attend to the responsibilities of family and ministry with nonstop commitment. Attending and participating in every worship service, funeral, Bible study, prayer. Administrating, planning for the ministry, meeting while mentoring the next generation of ministers and staff. Attending to the needs of my extensive and busy family. As demanding as everything was, I kept going, believing this was part of my calling.

Suddenly, I found myself having disagreements both at home and with members of the church. The stress caused me to pull back. I realized I needed a pause. It was time to refocus. Time to enter a Sabbath rest (see Leviticus 23:3).

Everybody depended on "the Reverend Sheila." They knew I would show up. Family and friends loved me, they cared about me and wanted me to be there for them, and I felt the same way. However, I had become worn out. Physically, mentally, and emotionally, I could not move forward or backward, found myself frozen, and heard my soul crying out *stop*—and I did.

I did the only thing I knew to do. As the hymn writer wrote, "I [went] to the garden alone," in prayer. I found myself in a selah moment, a pause. The Holy Spirit made me realize life and church were going to continue on, no matter what state of mental or physical being I found myself in. Giving myself permission to stop and minister to my needs brought an instant sense of relief—a shift. I remember feeling relaxed and confident as I submitted my sabbatical letter. I gained satisfaction in caring for my soul. Acknowledging I belonged to God, I knew that if I were to serve Him effectively, I had to first help myself: rest, then, became a form of praise and worship unto Him.

In my soul-care moment, I realized I could not return to the same method of serving Him as I had in previous decades. It was time for a renewed calling, and I began to feel a new appreciation for my calling and testimony.

Reflection

What rewards do you experience when you pause to care for your own soul?

May each of us thrive, to be well physically, mentally, emotionally, and spiritually, to be an effective witness for Him. Ultimately, a selah is rewarding. Its rewards are . . . quality time with the Lord without interruption. Being in the mental place He wants us to be in, so that we can hear His voice. A pause allowing us to reflect on our weaknesses and strengths, to renew our spirit, mind, and soul, and to receive wisdom for the work ahead.

During my selah, God awakened my heart and mind to the ways He's worked throughout my life, and He's given me renewed energy and strength to continue to serve for His glory. Having received these gifts through my time of selah, now I encourage you: Make space—give yourself permission—to care for your soul.

Hebrews 4:14–16

[14] Therefore, since we have a great high priest who has ascended into heaven, Jesus the Son of God, let us hold firmly to the faith we profess. [15] For we do not have a high priest who is unable to empathize with our weaknesses, but we have one who has been tempted in every way, just as we are—yet he did not sin. [16] Let us then approach God's throne of grace with confidence, so that we may receive mercy and find grace to help us in our time of need.

Release and Refill

But Martha was distracted by all
the preparations that had to be made.

LUKE 10:40

I had no idea I had neglected to fill my soul. As a speaker and therapist, God had prepared me through education, experience, and the opportunity to work in every sector of mental health. As a professor, with gratitude, I help students uncover their gifts and talents. We share moments in each other's lives, and experience vulnerability and strength together. Even with these humbling experiences, there remained a hollowness and void in my life.

I sometimes mirror the behaviors of Martha, busy with distractions while God is in the midst (see Luke 10:38–42). My life revolves around rushing from point A to point B, without taking time to live in the moment and experience God's goodness, grace, and mercy. In addition to my career, I am a wife, mother, foster parent, auntie, sister, friend, Soror, and *Sister Thornton*. I often feel as if I have to squeeze everything onto my calendar and still say yes even when my calendar says no. I squeeze in morning devotions, exercise, and, to keep it real, husband, children, and doctor appointments. However, the more I do, the more distant I feel from God. Emptiness. And the feeling that God is not pleased with me. I'm busy doing, like our sister Martha did even with Jesus in her midst.

During some of my speaking engagements, I provide attendees with bracelets encouraging them to *let go and let God*. Retreat provides me the opportunity to find answers to my questions and to pause—to really let go and let God. When I eliminate the distractions, unplug from technology, turn off my brain, and stop trying to control and schedule every aspect of my life, I experience peace! A calmness sweeps over my body. I do not feel guilty for taking time for me. I hear God speak to my spirit.

On the third morning of a fall retreat, I awoke with these words repeatedly playing in my head: "For I know the plans I have for you" (Jeremiah 29:11). This resonated with my soul! God was speaking to me during my pause from a reality filled with events, appointments, and activities. I listened. Yes, the drain, the void, the emptiness came from serving self instead of God. Ironically, during my presentation, I stressed that God cannot fill a vessel that is already full. Yet, I had filled my own vessel with things that I thought were important instead of letting God fill it.

As women, many of us go through life trying to fill areas that only God can fill, trying to control

Reflection

Does my busyness resemble yours? What are you busy doing? When was the last time that you simply paused?

things that only God can control or fix. We become full of the stuff we're not supposed to be carrying anyway. But when we release those things and sit at the feet of our Lord (like Mary), we can get full of God and what God will fill us with. In fact, the emptier we are, the more we can be filled with God. We can align with God, trust Him with our whole heart, and *let go and let God*. God, free us from any guilt we feel for taking time for You.

Luke 10:38–42

[38] As Jesus and his disciples were on their way, he came to a village where a woman named Martha opened her home to him. [39] She had a sister called Mary, who sat at the Lord's feet listening to what he said. [40] But Martha was distracted by all the preparations that had to be made. She came to him and asked, "Lord, don't you care that my sister has left me to do the work by myself? Tell her to help me!"

[41] "Martha, Martha," the Lord answered, "you are worried and upset about many things, [42] but few things are needed—or indeed only one. Mary has chosen what is better, and it will not be taken away from her."

Barbara L. Peacock

I Need Still

Be still, and know that I am God;
I will be exalted among the nations,
I will be exalted in the earth.

PSALM 46:10

In the midst of inundated schedules, important appointments, and overextended lives, the call to *be* and the call to *do* remain. Therein lies a tension, however; the necessity of *being* takes precedence over the demands of *doing*. In God's divine nature, He created human *beings* versus human *do*-ings. Too often, women are launched out into the vastness of the world before we are adequately equipped with the understanding that *being* in Christ sustains our soul for life's journey.

I suffered a "dark night of the soul" in my life—a time of spiritual bleakness, anxiety, and depression. Some call this being in "a dry place." I discovered that my antidote was soul care. I was serving in a mega ministry: praying, teaching, preaching, counseling, mentoring . . . you get the picture: *doing*. Even though I was giving and serving tremendously, my soul was not being effectively replenished. I thank God that it was a short season and when I came out, once again I was excited to get out of my bed versus stay in a fetal position facing a wall.

In Psalm 46:10, the Lord encouraged His chosen Hebrew people, "*Be* still and know that I am God" (emphasis added). The Lord saw the challenges they were experiencing and assured them of His sovereign capability and care. His desire was to protect them amid turmoil and calamities. Wars were raging, nations were in an uproar, and kingdoms were falling. The circumstances surrounding them did not intimidate Almighty God. He simply called them to a position of knowing trust in Him; not a suggestion but a command. Such a command is for our everyday lives and tumultuous times of overt warfare (Exodus 14:14).

Regardless of the challenges of life and the immensity of our commitments, God likewise calls us to embrace His care with confidence. He assures us that the assignments He predesigned for us to do and accomplish will be fulfilled. He wants us to fully trust and depend on Him.

In stillness, vision is birthed, peace prevails, and striving ceases. His care allows us to completely surrender body, soul, and spirit. Stillness sets the atmosphere to experience God's intimate presence.

Reflection

Will you join me and say as well, "I need still"? Pray: Dear God, I'm humbled that You desire intimacy with me. Please forgive me for allowing the circumstances of life to take precedence over my sacred time with You. I surrender all to You.

Even now, take a pause. Selah! Embrace His loving arms as He wraps you closely in His comfort. Listen to His heartbeat as you let go of the difficulties of life that so easily distract. In His loving arms, we are safe. It is here that we regain strength to complete the journey He has called and predestined specifically for each one of us.

Even though I have healed over time, daily I am mindful to practice the discipline of stillness. I need to be still.

Psalm 46 (NKJV)

¹ God is our refuge and strength,

A very present help in trouble.

² Therefore we will not fear,

Even though the earth be removed,

And though the mountains be carried into the midst of
        the sea;

³ Though its waters roar and be troubled,

Though the mountains shake with its swelling. *Selah*

⁴ There is a river whose streams shall make glad the city
        of God,

The holy place of the tabernacle of the Most High.

⁵ God is in the midst of her, she shall not be moved;

God shall help her, just at the break of dawn.

⁶ The nations raged, the kingdoms were moved;

He uttered His voice, the earth melted.

⁷ The LORD of hosts is with us;

The God of Jacob is our refuge. *Selah*

⁸ Come, behold the works of the LORD,
Who has made desolations in the earth.
⁹ He makes wars cease to the end of the earth;
He breaks the bow and cuts the spear in two;
He burns the chariot in the fire.

¹⁰ Be still, and know that I am God;
I will be exalted among the nations,
I will be exalted in the earth!

¹¹ The LORD of hosts is with us;
The God of Jacob is our refuge. *Selah*

Super Soul Soothing

Come to me, all you who are weary
and heavy burdened, and I will give you rest.

MATTHEW 11:28

There was a swing on the balcony that overlooked palm trees, a pool, and the beach. The hotel bathroom was so large it included double vanities and make-up mirrors, a walk-in shower, a tub, and an enclosed toilet. Wow! God used the retreat director to persistently encourage me to attend an exclusive retreat and made it a discounted opportunity I could not refuse. The combination of free time, fellowship, activities, and presenters were a healing balm I needed more than I'd realized. God did exceedingly, abundantly above what I could ask or imagine (Ephesians 3:20).

During the workshop for caregivers, involuntary tears flooded my face in a steady stream after the facilitator shared a beautiful opening message that ended with two simple words, "Thank you." It was extremely soothing to my soul because I had often felt unappreciated, emotionally wounded, and weary in my work as a caregiver for my mom, who had a sudden stroke years earlier and, since then, declining health. My God orchestrated this divine opportunity where I was able to exhale and experience rest, restoration, revival, and renewal. Part of my reluctance of going on the retreat had been the responsibility of finding temporary care for my mom. After I released my resistance, God provided home-care coverage for my mom. And I gratefully heeded God's call to come and retreat and pause.

A retreat is not always accompanied by a balcony and swing and soaking tub, though. Another selah shift occurred during the first full week of the year, when my church implements its annual consecration. During this time, the congregation is asked to fast and pray, which includes eating one meal per day and attending one-hour prayer services at the church. This year's fast led me to be consistent in new spiritual practices. During the consecration, I woke up before daybreak to pray and meditate; and I was guided to some YouTube videos that gave me a deeper understanding of prayer and fasting. I also started reading *The One Year Bible* again and wrote down thoughts of what resonated with me as I read the daily passages. I felt encouraged by how, despite their poor decisions, God worked all things together for the good of Abraham, Isaac, Jacob, Joseph, and the many other godly men and women, because they loved Him and were called according to His purpose (Romans 8:28).

After the consecration, I was inspired to continue fasting one day per week because Jesus said some situations can only be fixed by prayer *and* fasting (Mark 9:29 NKJV). I also downloaded the Daily Audio Bible app to my phone for the option of listening to—as well as reading—the Bible; and I listened to YouTube videos of Bible stories, Scriptures, affirmations, prayers, and meditations to help me sleep soundly and wake up in gratitude and joy. The combination of these spiritual practices and the positive results that manifest from them have grown and strengthened my faith and confidence.

My mind and soul bask in God's peace because I engage in these selah *rest-in-God* moments as Jesus did when He often stole away from the crowds and His disciples. Jesus knew the importance of shifting to time alone to commune with our Father God, and He received the power, wisdom, and guidance to endure to the end. How much more is the need for us? To make *and* take time to soothe our souls on a continual basis is vital for our overall well-being. You can't always leave town or afford to resort. But we can always steal away and take time for reflection and rest with our Lord.

Reflection

How have you been caring for your soul, and in what ways have your efforts been effective?

Luke 22:39–43

39 Jesus went out as usual to the Mount of Olives, and his disciples followed him. 40 On reaching the place, he said to them, "Pray that you will not fall into temptation." 41 He withdrew about a stone's throw beyond them, knelt down and prayed, 42 "Father, if you are willing, take this cup from me; yet not my will, but yours be done." 43 An angel from heaven appeared to him and strengthened him.

His Perfect Plans

"Not by might nor by power, but by my Spirit,"
says the LORD Almighty.

ZECHARIAH 4:6

After I surrendered my life to the Lord during one amazing week in Sydney, Australia, I came back home to New York a different person. I couldn't explain what was happening to me at the time, but looking back now, I see that God was slowly transforming and conforming me into the image of His Son. I suddenly found myself wanting to go to church and interested in reading the Bible. As I learned more about Jesus, my life started to change. My circle of friends changed. How I dressed changed. What I did with my free time changed. Even the music I listened to and the jokes I laughed at changed.

It's not that I was a horrible person or that someone was telling me I had to stop everything. The more I spent time with God, the more I realized I had been living far from Him for too long.

Still, I wasn't ready for what the Lord would ask me to change next. I was stunned when I felt the Lord calling me to lay down my journalism career. That was all I had studied and worked in. I had no clue what to do next, but I knew I needed to follow God's lead.

That started me on a journey that included teaching middle-school English at a Christian school for a year and doing communications work at a nonprofit for several years. I also took classes at a Bible school and went on short-term mission trips to five countries.

When I would read about how God asked Moses to drop his rod and then pick it up (Exodus 4:2–5), I started to feel that God would one day call me to pick up my pen to write for His glory. But I didn't know what that could look like. My public writing career had lain dormant for so long. I fussed and fretted while trying to figure out what I should be doing. I felt like Peter, anxiously waiting to be called out of the boat to walk on water (Matthew 14:28).

I soon learned that God wasn't in a hurry. He would gently remind me that anything I might accomplish for Him would not be in my own strength, but in His perfect timing and way. One of the verses that followed me like surround sound was, "'Not by might nor by power, but by my Spirit,' says the LORD Almighty" (Zechariah 4:6). I finally realized God wanted me to remain at rest in Him instead of being consumed by all the good works I thought He had for me to do.

As we abide in Christ and sit at His feet as Mary did (Luke 10:39), our heart is aligned with God. We can be at peace with His perfect plans for us. May we rejoice in seeking God above all else. "But seek first his kingdom and his righteousness, and all these things will be given to you as well" (Matthew 6:33).

Reflection

Are you resting and at peace knowing that God is in control of every aspect of your life and future?

• • •

How can seeking God first help to realign you and give you peace?

Matthew 6:25–34

[25] "Therefore I tell you, do not worry about your life, what you will eat or drink; or about your body, what you will wear. Is not life more than food, and the body more than clothes? [26] Look at the birds of the air; they do not sow or reap or store away in barns, and yet your heavenly Father feeds them. Are you not much more valuable than they? [27] Can any one of you by worrying add a single hour to your life?

[28] "And why do you worry about clothes? See how the flowers of the field grow. They do not labor or spin. [29] Yet I tell you that not even Solomon in all his splendor was dressed like one of these. [30] If that is how God clothes the grass of the field, which is here today and tomorrow is thrown into the fire, will he not much more clothe you—you of little faith? [31] So do not worry, saying, 'What shall we eat?' or 'What shall we drink?' or 'What shall we wear?' [32] For the pagans run after all these things, and your heavenly Father knows that you need them. [33] But seek first his kingdom and his righteousness, and all these things will be given to you as well. [34] Therefore do not worry about tomorrow, for tomorrow will worry about itself. Each day has enough trouble of its own."

Metamorphic

I'm drained

Feels like I'm swimming upstream

My life is changing in ways that seem diametrically opposed
     to the indoctrinations of my

youth

I'm uneasy

Expectant

I really need a hug

My life is shifting in ways that feel simultaneously disrespectful
     and yet somehow

liberating

It was so easy to go against the grain for others

To protect their right to be themselves, free and unfettered
     within the will of God

It was so easy to support them and undergird their dreams
     and midwife their aspirations

And, yet, the pain of birthing myself into who I am—who I
am called to be—is almost

unbearable

You see, the floodgates have opened . . .

A dam has broken

The currents are swift

The rapids are turbulent

The waters converge into a single channel

The pains of the past no longer safely imprisoned behind lock
and key

The reality of horrors once shut away

The betrayals of those who themselves were once betrayed

The knowledge of my own culpability—who knew I had the
power for change . . .

I'm tried

I'm drained

Feels like I'm swimming upstream

My life is changing in ways that boggle my mind and challenge my soul

Emotionally, I'm spent

Physically, I'm drained

Intellectually, I know that I am on the right path

Spiritually, I trust God

I step back to regroup

I step back to refresh

I step back for a moment to let my "me" digest the cata-
strophic yet, metamorphic impact

of change

Inevitable . . .

Indelible . . .

Irreversible . . . change

Stepping back to regroup

Stepping back to refresh

Stepping back to gain clarity

Stepping back, to let God be God

In peace

I will lie down and sleep,

for you alone, LORD,

make me dwell in safety.

PSALM 4:8

Safe-Space Sisterhood

I love to hear Vickie Winans sing "Safe in His Arms." As she sings, one can feel the warmth, the holy hug, the safety net, as perhaps some girls felt in our earthly dad's arms when we were little. But the song is sung to our heavenly Father, and is about how we long to feel, as children of the most high God.

And when you are a woman who arrives at or who makes time for your selah, it's because your heart, along with those of all the other women who may be present, is longing to find both the warmth of the Father's presence, and the safe, sacred space of sisterhood. So we gather with our sisters from both near and far.

There is a code, not one of silence, but of trust, that what we do, say, and share is sacred. That for the time we are together, we are experiencing the triune God—and we are joint heirs to the throne (Romans 8:17). There is a holy royalty, a sister "thing" that emerges. In this room, in this sacred space, is the sister I've been waiting for, and she's been waiting for me.

As the title of the once popular movie suggests, we collectively exhale. We are no longer waiting. When we arrive at retreat rest, we breathe in Jesus, and breathe out the Holy Spirit. All year long, we are working, serving, and caring for families, sometimes our own and other times others'. We're expending energy for congregations, businesses, classes, and parents. And then, finally, there's time for *me*! That's sacred. And to be able to share it with someone else, whose needs are similar to mine, that's sacred. So we make room for this.

Psalm 42 describes what I feel the most as we gather together: "As the deer pants for streams of water, so my soul pants for you, my God" (v. 1). In my sisters, I see the love of God, the beauty of God, and the wonder of God. God, we pant after Thee. We are thirsty for selah. It is our sacred brook, our sacred space. And our thirst is quenched. The panting stops and the praise begins.

—*Suzan D. Johnson Cook*

Safe in Her Arms

When Elizabeth heard Mary's greeting, the baby leaped
in her womb, and Elizabeth was filled with the Holy Spirit.
In a loud voice she exclaimed:
"Blessed are you among women,
and blessed is the child you will bear!"

LUKE 1:41–42

It was a hard week. I found myself emotionally drained. I could not wait to get to the annual retreat for women who desperately need to pause and reflect. As if the pressure of being a new pastor weren't enough, I now wrestled with the recent discovery of a cancerous mass found on my ninety-one-year-old mother-in-law's lung—that had doubled in size within the previous month. This diagnosis was followed by the recommendation that no one wants to hear: hospice care. I was devastated.

Have you ever received a diagnosis so severe, information so terrible, or a task so great it overwhelms you to the point of wanting to escape? Well, that was me. I was no longer retreating. I was *escaping*.

I wonder if this was how young Mary felt after receiving the divine diagnosis that she would give birth to the Savior of the world? This incredible revelation and the overwhelming sense of responsibility fueled her great need to escape and retreat with Elizabeth, her seasoned and wise cousin, who knew all too well the pressure of carrying that which has the power to change the world and rock yours. However, can you imagine the relief and overwhelming sense of comfort Mary must have felt when she arrived at Elizabeth's home? The older woman greeted her with cries of blessings and honor in her time of uncertainty and transition.

In my season of uncertainty and transition, I found my own Elizabeth in the person of a dear sister. One look at me as I walked into our retreat space and she wordlessly opened her arms. She held me as I melted and cried. I cried for the workload I was carrying. I cried for my mother-in-law. I cried for the husband I had to stay strong for. And I cried in relief because I had found a safe space in the arms of a seasoned, wise woman who also understood all too well the pressure of being chosen by God to carry that which has the power to change the world.

Like Mary, every woman needs an Elizabeth. You also may have the opportunity to be *Elizabeth* to a sister who has an overwhelming need to escape. And when she does share that need, make sure to keep your door and your arms open.

Opening begins with opening one's heart, for that is where true, unconditional love begins. One of the reasons to do one-on-one, face-to-face conference calls with one another is to *see* how we're doing. So many mistakenly think that when we're asked to introduce ourselves in a setting that people are impressed with *who* we are. In keeping the door and arms open, we show one another *how* we are.

Nowhere in the world will people ever be the same after this virus trauma that has sickened millions, shattered dreams, halted weddings, eliminated events, canceled out corporations, and more.

When I was a kid and folks would be diagnosed with cancer, they wouldn't say the word, they'd just say "the big C," and everyone knew what they were referring to. These days, all one has to say is "the virus," and everyone will know what you're speaking about.

We are all affected and impacted by it. There will be many Marys coming into the spaces where you are, trying to find a place off the beaten path, seeking a sister whose arms and heart are open. That means before they even come, we must prepare our hearts and our minds, and be determined to be in a state of readiness. For they will need steadiness. Can you be the Elizabeth in the room, the one who is so connected to the Spirit that the possibilities inside of you leap when you greet each other, knowing you're in the right place with the right sister, and you're right on time?

Luke 1:39–45

[39] At that time Mary got ready and hurried to a town in the hill country of Judea, [40] where she entered

Reflection

Who can you run to? Pray and ask God to provide someone in your life with whom you can retreat. Then, ask God for the opportunity to be that safe space for someone else in the future.

Zechariah's home and greeted Elizabeth. [41] When Elizabeth heard Mary's greeting, the baby leaped in her womb, and Elizabeth was filled with the Holy Spirit. [42] In a loud voice she exclaimed: "Blessed are you among women, and blessed is the child you will bear! [43] But why am I so favored, that the mother of my Lord should come to me? [44] As soon as the sound of your greeting reached my ears, the baby in my womb leaped for joy. [45] Blessed is she who has believed that the Lord would fulfill his promises to her!"

Sweet and Complete

Why, my soul, are you downcast?
Why so disturbed within me?
Put your hope in God, for I will yet praise him,
my Savior and my God.

PSALM 43:5

Have you ever longed for a safe space? A place where you could go to find peace and rest. A place where you could be exactly who you were meant to be. A place where you would not be judged. A place described in Scripture as so full of peace that it is beyond your understanding (Philippians 4:4–7).

If I were to give that place a name, it might be called *contentment*. We as sisters put so much time and energy into building all we aspire to be. We're so driven and yet once the dream is achieved, there remains a void. That void must be addressed if we are to know and experience contentment. It's no wonder the psalmist questioned why his soul was cast down and disquieted (Psalm 43:5). When we prioritize things of lesser meaning above ourselves, this is the end result.

When we neglect ourselves, and our God-given needs, we forget . . .

- to discover who we really are as individuals;

- to realize how uniquely we are designed;

- to experience the joy that no other individual, anywhere, is like the beautiful person we see in the mirror.

The only way to get to this place of contentment is to remove false appearances. Let's take off the mask of wanting to be something we are not. The mask we wear for those we most want to impress, who may not understand our need for soul care. There are sisters in high places who want the opportunity to be transparent. They would admit that despite all of their accomplishments, when alone with their thoughts, they feel like Solomon. He wrote, "I have seen all the works that are done under the sun; and, behold, all is vanity and vexation of spirit" (Ecclesiastes 1:14 KJV). This, spoken by the wisest man in Scripture! He was looking at life, and because of the wisdom he possessed, he could see human life in its true nature.

There comes a time when we must be proactive: to act in anticipation of future problems, needs, or changes. More than ever, we need a safe space, and once found, it must be protected. This means that we will need to do an evaluation of our life's activities, of the things that drain us or that are life-giving to us. From that evaluation, we can begin to let go of some things—and some people—to protect our peace of mind. It's possible that you find yourself in a situation where you may feel things will never change. But you must realize that if the situation does not change, then you can change in the situation.

You can devise a plan to assist you as you experience a season of pain or distress. It reminds me of the stanza in "My Hope Is Built on Nothing Less" that states, "When all around my soul gives way, he then is all my hope and stay."

Our Lord has made a promise no one else can keep; He will never leave us or forsake us. He will be there through the rough places, and, if you seek Him, you will find Him. At some point, we may have to follow David's example. During a low season in his life, when he was all alone, he encouraged himself in the Lord. If we as a body of sisters are able to find that safe space in God, the rest of this journey called life will be sweet and complete.

> ## Reflection
>
> *What ways will you commit to having a safe space to protect your peace and to thrive?*

Philippians 4:4–7

[4] Rejoice in the Lord always. I will say it again: Rejoice! [5] Let your gentleness be evident to all. The Lord is near. [6] Do not be anxious about anything, but in every situation, by prayer and petition, with thanksgiving, present your requests to God. [7] And the peace of God, which transcends all understanding, will guard your hearts and your minds in Christ Jesus.

Genuine

Don't just pretend to love others.
Really love them. Hate what is wrong.
Hold tightly to what is good.

ROMANS 12:9 (NLT)

*I*n the fashion world, we search for specific labels to authenticate products, assuring ourselves that we are getting the genuine article. Some of us won't accept anything but a genuine leather handbag or a designer dress suit. Yet, when it comes to our fellowship with each other, we know we need to be even more particular about being authentic.

An early church leader, the apostle known as Paul reminds Christian believers of our responsibility to be concerned not only with our devotion and fellowship with God, but also with each other (Romans 12:9).

We are instructed as believers, as sisters in Christ, to live a life of genuine love for God, as well as for each other. The verse in Romans outlines this simple reminder: love others without pretense. No hypocrisy—no pretending—no masks that give a false impression of genuine concern. We need to be in true, loving fellowship as Christian believers, as sisters, and as women who serve. It is genuine love that makes the difference in our interactions with each other. We make room for it in our hearts and relationships.

Genuine love cannot be bought or sold. It is only to be given freely out of the depth of our love for the Lord. Jesus's death on the cross displayed genuine love. Out of this love, we can pursue God's call to us to love one another through His strength that flows in and through us. We will never be able to come close to Jesus's demonstration of love for us, but we can press toward the high calling to love one another. We can all have genuine love and fellowship with our sisters (and brothers). Let's ask the Lord to give us a deeper understanding of the sacredness of genuine fellowship. Let's pray that He teaches us *how to hold tightly to the genuine good* in our relationships with our sisters. Fellowshiping also provides us a moment to pause and celebrate each other and God's goodness to us; there can truly be rest, peace, and wholeness in fellowshiping with those we love and cherish.

Reflection

Think about a relationship you cherish. How are you demonstrating God's love?

1 John 4:7–21

[7] Dear friends, let us love one another, for love comes from God. Everyone who loves has been born of God and knows God. [8] Whoever does not love does not know God, because God is love. [9] This is how God showed his love among us: He sent his one and only Son into the world that we might live through him. [10] This is love: not that we loved God, but that he loved

us and sent his Son as an atoning sacrifice for our sins. ¹¹ Dear friends, since God so loved us, we also ought to love one another. ¹² No one has ever seen God; but if we love one another, God lives in us and his love is made complete in us.

¹³ This is how we know that we live in him and he in us: He has given us of his Spirit. ¹⁴ And we have seen and testify that the Father has sent his Son to be the Savior of the world. ¹⁵ If anyone acknowledges that Jesus is the Son of God, God lives in them and they in God. ¹⁶ And so we know and rely on the love God has for us.

God is love. Whoever lives in love lives in God, and God in them. ¹⁷ This is how love is made complete among us so that we will have confidence on the day of judgment: In this world we are like Jesus. ¹⁸ There is no fear in love. But perfect love drives out fear, because fear has to do with punishment. The one who fears is not made perfect in love.

¹⁹ We love because he first loved us. ²⁰ Whoever claims to love God yet hates a brother or sister is a liar. For whoever does not love their brother and sister, whom they have seen, cannot love God, whom they have not seen. ²¹ And he has given us this command: Anyone who loves God must also love their brother and sister.

Friends in Grace

Sweet friendships refresh the soul
and awaken our hearts with joy,
for good friends are like the anointing oil
that yields the fragrant incense of God's presence.

PROVERBS 27:9 (TPT)

We have been friends since first grade. Because our last names started with the same letter, we found ourselves standing in line together, and seated near each other. A smile and a wave later, we began saving seats at lunch. Camaraderie grew as we teamed up for dodgeball at recess. At sleepovers, recovering from peals of laughter, we finally fell asleep close to dawn. We were close, literally and figuratively.

Our friendship of over fifty years began because of how close we were to one another situationally, and with all we held in common, as we were in the same class.

Elementary school was a breeze. Middle school was all-consuming. High school was punctuated with cheerleading, debate and drama, and graduating top ten. Three husbands and several lovers have known us. Six children between us, two miscarriages, and one abortion. She is a career office administrator—fulfilling girlhood dreams of the glamorous life of an executive secretary. I am a career religious practitioner—fulfilling girlhood dreams of preaching, teaching, and writing about the gospel. In spite of trajectories that kept her living within ten miles of her childhood home and those that afforded me opportunities to live in six states, we remain friends. We connect when I visit home, on social media, at high school reunions, and on occasions of grieving loved ones.

The Bible says, "A friend loves at all times, and a [sister] is born for a time of adversity" (Proverbs 17:17).

Through it all, I regard her as a part of me and evidence of God's grace. We learned the value of women friendships and endearing memories, and while we knew a lot of people by name, we made efforts to befriend and be friends. In her I found a safe space to grow up and grow into myself. I believe she received the same from me. A sweet friendship beginning with a wave, a smile, and laughter still thrives.

I more so attribute our meeting to that grace. Isn't that just how God does things? Places people in our paths and lives, and places us in the paths and lives of others. It's not a coincidence. It's providence that produces lifelong friends. Lifelong sharing. Lifelong stories.

As grown women—years of life experiences beyond the carefree innocence of girlhood—making friends can seem a mysterious, exhausting, and dreadful thing on our to-do list. We see each other coming and going, on the same commute, in shared residential spaces. We take note of hair, clothes, shoes, and commuter bags. While on our commute or through our mutual connections, we learn fragments of each other's stories.

We retreat to our corners of the elevators, staring at the ceiling; or feign urgent engagement with our phones, avoiding social expectations to acknowledge another in close quarters. Being a grown woman is likely a busy life; and is often a lonely life. We want friends but making grown-women friends eludes our pace of life.

Today, let's begin a revival of sweet friendships fragrant with God's presence in whom we live and move and have our being (Proverbs 27:9). Might you be the grace of God in another woman's life, just because you share so much in common; perhaps your faith, perhaps a smile. May you be a safe space for each other; and be sister-friends, walking, talking, and living in God.

Acts 17:25–28

[25] And he is not served by human hands, as if he needed anything. Rather, he himself gives everyone life and breath and everything else. [26] From one man he made all the nations, that they should inhabit the whole earth; and he marked out their appointed times in history and the boundaries of their lands. [27] God did this so that they would seek him and perhaps reach out for him and find

Reflection

Who is she—who is that woman you see all of the time to whom you will open the door to sweet friendship?

• • •

What sister-friendship from your past do you need to revive, renewing your bonds over shared faith?

him, though he is not far from any one of us. [28] 'For in him we live and move and have our being.' As some of your own poets have said, 'We are his offspring.'"

Beautiful Massage

Then he got up and rebuked the winds and the waves,
and it was completely calm.

MATTHEW 8:26

I've been living in two cities—Oakland, California, and New Orleans, Louisiana. My husband is pastor of the oldest Baptist church in all of Oakland, Beth Eden Baptist, the "Mother Church." Being "first lady" parent to four adult sons (one about to be married at this writing), planner for family and friends, grandmother of four, teacher of massage therapy, and a licensed practicing massage therapist in New Orleans (we're the number-one spa in the city, with a house filled with people for Mardi Gras)—I'm not complaining, but I have a *lot* on my plate. I'd even dare to say a smorgasbord! And I still find time to serve at retreats.

There's a beauty in massage—and I share it at retreats. Of the many reasons to get a massage: it relieves stress, reduces anxiety, boosts immunity, improves balance, and my favorite is that it promotes *relaxation*. Massage is good medicine. That's why I love what I do.

While I work on and with others to ensure they have a quality self-care moment, I always must make sure *I* have self-care space for myself. When I'm able to reflect on my time at retreat, I'm refreshed just with the thought of what I've experienced. It's a time of pause and refreshment for the busy woman, the Christian woman. Whether I am working on the sisters, or just conversing and sharing with them in fellowship and sister sessions, I feel *grounded*. I need my sisters. We need one another.

Reflection

What do you hear when you experience self-care in God's presence?

• • •

How do you let go to listen and live?

In our lives of moving fast from one thing to another, or during the times when life feels stressful, as though we're walking on a tightrope with no safety net, we need to gain some balance. We need support. Just being by the sea is refreshing, making time to sit in the water, taking time to pause. Not only do we need to pause during a retreat but also to continue to pause when returning home. I hear the words of Jesus echoing in my ear, when He was speaking to the roaring seas, "Peace, be still" (Mark 4:39 KJV). I think of all that's going on around me as roaring seas. And sometimes my life—the boat—is tossing, but I'm reminded to experience selah: to pause. Just as I ask those I give therapy to relax physically, I also need to pause spiritually. As I journal every day, I say to myself in my daily meditation, *I am calm, I am centered, I am balanced, I am happy. I trust You, God. I trust in Your control of the universe, and I let go.*

Matthew 8:23–27

²³ Then he got into the boat and his disciples followed him. ²⁴ Suddenly a furious storm came up on the lake, so that the waves swept over the boat. But Jesus was sleeping. ²⁵ The disciples went and woke him, saying, "Lord, save us! We're going to drown!"

²⁶ He replied, "You of little faith, why are you so afraid?" Then he got up and rebuked the winds and the waves, and it was completely calm.

²⁷ The men were amazed and asked, "What kind of man is this? Even the winds and the waves obey him!"

Selah

His splendor covers the heavens,

And the earth is full of His praise.

HABAKKUK 3:3 (NASB)

Starting Over

*O*ur seasons in life can be beautiful or painful, but they do not linger. Just as spring must move over for summer, and summer hails down fall, and then old man winter says, "It's getting cold up in here," there are seasons of life. One makes room for the next. To everything, there is a season, a time for each moment and movement in our lives (see Ecclesiastes 3). Scripture declares there is a time to be born, a time to die, a time to plant, and a time to pluck what we've planted (v. 2).

I've seen two generations of intergenerational, multicultural women leaders come through Selah retreats. We began as WIMIN (Women in Ministry International), a conference that boasted and hosted three hundred women ministers strong, who came to Fort Lauderdale, Florida. These were the early days of ministry for many women, and they just wanted to be in the same room with other women ministers.

When I became the first female president of the historic Hampton University Ministers' Conference and started the women in ministry hour, some twelve hundred women preachers would try to fill—pack—the room, squeezing in just to be able to touch and get a glimpse of other women like themselves. Many approached the front of the room before, during, and after the session, whispering and asking if I could mentor them. They were so excited and knew that some sort of answer was in that room. Some sort of new beginning.

I told them I couldn't mentor each one of them individually, but collectively I could gather my friends and sister colleagues and put together a conference if they'd like to come. And come they did by planes, trains, cars, and buses. They came. And WIMIN was born.

But as seasons progressed and people's needs and lives changed, and as their ministries matured into their new seasons, it morphed into Selah by the Sea.

We started afresh with Christian women leaders in all arenas in ministry and in the marketplace, who needed that break, a pause, just like male preachers and pastors—and someone to help them to do it. We all are busy, but making time for ourselves and for ourselves with God sometimes takes some prodding. The Holy Spirit would not leave me alone. I was the "prodder," the provocateur, the one whom the Holy Spirit used to not leave the sisters alone.

Then the season changed again. We did not need three-hundred-plus in attendance and headliners on the stage to fill the room or fulfill or authenticate or validate us. So many judge the success of a conference by the numbers or the big names in attendance. And, yes, we had all that, yet we found the intimacy and the quality of the relationships, friendships, and sessions for sharing were immeasurable, as lives transformed in smaller, more intimate contexts.

Like the sister walking all alone on the beach, or the woman who put her foot in the ocean for the first time, or the one who sculpted a sandcastle, while another put on a bathing suit for the first time. Many just kept repeating, "Thank you, thank you, thank you." It was the small things, the simple things, the special things and times that really mattered. It was the move toward pause, stillness, reflection, and listening to the Lord that mattered.

The largest Christian church in the world—Yoido Full Gospel Church in Seoul, South Korea—began with two or three people praying at a time, all alone on bended knees in a prayer grotto, in a little hole in the mountains, in hills where there were no billboards, posters, or ad space, no social media or blogging, no choirs or earthly praise teams. Just women praying. Through them, God built the church into the sixty-thousand-plus membership. But the leaders said they weren't counting numbers or members. They were measuring success by the power of the Holy Spirit, and the impact of the prayers to God, the Holy return on investment.

"For where two or three gather in my name, there am I with them" (Matthew 18:20).

At this writing, many of the boomer generation are retiring or planning to retire, or reinventing, repositioning, or rebranding themselves for their latter decades or seasons.

So now, a new season emerges, and the younger women for whom earlier generations prayed, fought, advocated, and blazed trails are coming into their own new season. Their needs now in this season—as church, community, and business leaders; as wives, some as parents, and as all sorts of influencers—are different than when they were younger. With seasons of growth, they are able to share, not only with the generations who preceded them, but also with generations who follow them.

Seasons change. They will not wait for us. We must flow with them, renew with them, and prepare to renew. That's why being near and on the water reminds me, "Keep your flow as you grow." Like the waves, there will be ebbs and flows. No one can stop your season from happening. What can you do to be ready? How will you begin again? Watch God renew you as you take moments to pause and reflect and draw closer to Him.

—*Suzan D. Johnson Cook*

Getting Up Again

The godly may trip seven times, but they will get up again.
But one disaster is enough to overthrow the wicked.

PROVERBS 24:16 (NLT)

*A*ll of us at one time or another will face something that trips us up and almost takes us out. It could be a ministry disappointment, a broken relationship, a job promotion that never happened, a failed business attempt, or a family tragedy. Sometimes those things take the wind out of us, and we are walking wounded—fearing that we might never see a time of flourishing in our lives.

I have had a few things in my life that tripped me up and made me question my faith and my God. The premature birth of my second son at twenty-six weeks, the marriage crisis I went through at my ten-year point, and attempting to launch a church. All of these situations were different, but they all were able to bring me to my knees. Many times during those phases of my life, I didn't think I could make it out. I tripped on life. These situations almost made me get out of the ring and hang up my boxing gloves. But because of the everlasting love of God and His patience with me, I got up again, each and every time. Truth is, as daughters of the Most High God, we have that power, and it exists in our DNA. As the proverb says, one disaster can certainly take out those who do not know the Lord but not so for those of us who do (24:16). Resilience is an inherited trait from our divine makeup.

We live in a fallen world that is in captivity. Because of this reality, we will experience some major disappointments in life. While we are not promised an easy life as believers, we are promised that we will get up again. This implies that our get-up times will be numerous on this side of heaven. What a confidence booster to know that no matter how many times we trip because of life circumstances, we can get up!

Aside from our heavenly DNA that helps us get up after difficult moments, we also have to store up a few things in our body and soul. Start by putting *yourself* in your calendar. Take vacations, go out for walks, spend time with friends. All these practices also help us get up in times of trouble because of the rest and support they bring to our lives.

Woman of God, go forth in what you have been called to do knowing that no matter what comes your way, if it trips you up, you will get up! God does not care how many times we trip.

Reflection

Are you experiencing something that makes you feel defeated? How might reflecting on Scripture give you the confidence you need to get back up?

Habakkuk 3:17–19 (NASB)

¹⁷ Even if the fig tree does not blossom,
And there is no fruit on the vines,
If the yield of the olive fails,
And the fields produce no food,
Even if the flock disappears from the fold,
And there are no cattle in the stalls,
¹⁸ Yet I will triumph in the Lord,
I will rejoice in the God of my salvation.
¹⁹ The Lord God is my strength,
And He has made my feet like deer's feet,
And has me walk on my high places.

Damascus Road

But whatever were gains to me
I now consider loss for the sake of Christ.

PHILIPPIANS 3:7

As a child, I was captivated by the pageantry of the Olympics. I dreamed of traveling the world to meet my favorite Olympians and of experiencing all the sights and sounds surrounding the legendary Games.

I was so passionate about being among the elite athletes, that I set my heart and mind to pursue a journalism career and dreamed of going to the Olympics as a reporter. Within a few years, I had a master's degree in journalism from New York University, was working at a women's magazine in Times Square, and interviewing celebrities and famous athletes.

And after much hard work, to my great delight, I found myself at the Sydney Olympics as a reporter and spectator. I was on a mission to soak in all the grandeur of the Games during my one week there. I didn't know God was on a mission to chase me down all the way in Australia. I had been so focused on my career that I had grown further and further from God. Being in Sydney was a cross between my gold-medal moment and my road to Damascus.

I had a lovely time at the Olympics, but on my last day there, I found myself crying in Olympic park. Although I had achieved this great goal of mine, I still felt empty and dissatisfied. I still wanted more. *Why?*

That was when I realized I had come to the end of myself.

I thought about how I had tried to run my life without God.

In His great mercy, God had still let me accomplish so many of my dreams. I was so overwhelmed by God's love and grace that I looked up at the open sky and said, "I can't do anything else but serve you the rest of my life."

By His grace, I have been walking with the Lord ever since.

When I think back to that September in Sydney, I'm reminded of the apostle Paul and his dramatic first encounter with Jesus. Saul, as he was then known, was headed to Damascus bent on persecuting Christians (see Acts 9).

But God had other plans. Saul's transformation was astounding.

Saul, the persecutor of the early church, became the apostle Paul, who devoted the rest of his life to preaching the gospel. He was one of the first missionaries and wrote a majority of the New Testament (see Acts 26).

Although Paul had an impressive résumé before coming to Christ, he would later write, "But whatever were gains to me I now consider loss for the sake of Christ. What is more, I consider everything a loss because of the surpassing worth of knowing Christ Jesus my Lord, for whose sake I have lost all things. I consider them garbage, that I may gain Christ and be found in him, not having a righteousness of my own that comes from the law, but that which is through faith in Christ—the righteousness that comes from God on the basis of faith" (Philippians 3:7–9).

Paul understood there was nothing better than knowing God and living for Him.

God doesn't want us scheming and stressing to achieve worldly success. He wants us to take His yoke and learn of Him (Matthew 11:29).

Starting over and living for Christ can seem daunting at first. But we are called to follow His purposes for us—no matter what season we might be in or how many times it seems we are called to start over.

Reflection

How do you respond when you feel the Lord calling you to let go of your plans and to draw closer to Him??

Philippians 3:7–9

[7] But whatever were gains to me I now consider loss for the sake of Christ. [8] What is more, I consider everything a loss because of the surpassing worth of knowing Christ Jesus my Lord, for whose sake I have lost all things. I consider them garbage, that I may gain Christ [9] and be found in him, not having a righteousness of my own that comes from the law, but that which is through faith in Christ—the righteousness that comes from God on the basis of faith.

Takana L. Jefferson

Called to Sing

To my dear friend, . . .
whom I love in the truth.

3 JOHN 1

*A*s an officer and chaplain of the US Navy, I had been in the military for more than twenty-eight years. I knew on arrival to the retreat that I had found my sisters. Laughter, leadership, and legacy were among the themes as we dealt with self-care, soul care, taking siestas, and growing together. All of us were busy women, and all needed a retreat space. Sometimes we shared it collectively, and other times there were those precious moments alone with God.

Walking along the beach, being able to look at the beauty of God's creation—just witnessing the beauty of the Creator—were experiences my soul had longed for. I thought of Psalm 8 and God's beautiful creations. I realized I needed the opportunity for renewal, and I received it in those moments reflecting on nature. I felt the breeze blow through my locks, reminding me of the Holy Spirit, and sensed God fill my soul. I started humming and began to sing the refrain to that great hymn, "Then sings my soul, . . . how great thou art." That described what I was feeling. In those moments, I could sense God's voice speaking softly to remind me *You are safe, and never alone because I am always with you.* It allowed me the time to rest my mind. As military, we are always *on call*, but in the quiet, I could revisit my call from God.

Sitting with my sisters, seeing God's beauty, and resting refreshed my soul, encouraged me to know that I have a refuge always, not only in a time of trouble—that I'm safe in His arms.

Reflection

When was the last time you took time alone with creation?

Are you making yourself a priority? How are you making God a priority? Isn't it time for a selah?

3 John 1–4

[1] To my dear friend, . . . whom I love in the truth.

[2] Dear friend, I pray that you may enjoy good health and that all may go well with you, even as your soul is getting along well. [3] It gave me great joy when some believers came and testified about your faithfulness to the truth, telling how you continue to walk in it. [4] I have no greater joy than to hear that my children are walking in the truth.

— *Martha Taylor LaCroix* —

The Unexpected Selah

This poor man cried out, and the LORD heard him,
and saved him out of all his troubles.

PSALM 34:6 (NKJV)

It was three a.m. Suffering from sleep deprivation, I could not seem to rest. I decided to sit alone in the lobby of my hotel in Copenhagen. I then began to write the summary of the previous day's accomplishments.

In the midst of a lively group of partygoers, a young man, uninvited, came and sat at my table. He had been drinking and his behavior was obnoxious. "What are you writing?" he asked, slurring as he spoke. For some reason, I did not feel impelled to answer. Nor did I look up in reaction to his rude behavior. With pen in my right hand, I continued to write. With my left, I handed him information about my organization. The brochure spoke of suicide prevention with a list of facts on the subject. I had traveled to Copenhagen to enroll European countries in our cause to reduce suicide by at least five percent per year globally.

He slowly stood up as he continued to read; then suddenly plopped back down in his chair. In a loud voice he said, "Thank you!"

This caused me to stop writing and look directly in his eyes. *Thank me for what?* I thought. He wanted to know more details of this work, so I began to do what he considered to be an elevator speech! Shouting from the top of his lungs, he said, "I don't wanna hear all that #@!#$!; talk to me straight up!" I suddenly froze! I stopped. I sensed that this young man was hurting and desperate for a raw, honest conversation. "This poor man cried out, and the LORD heard him, and saved him out of all his troubles," says Psalm 34:6 (NKJV).

Selah became real to me that morning in this way: through my need to pause and reflect on what has just been said. This is exactly what I had to do—and get present and mindful of the absolute disgust this young man was feeling toward himself and life. As I paused, I was then able to expose the guarded places of my heart and share pure vulnerabilities of my own experience.

I was curious as to why this nineteen-year-old young man said, "Thank you." He shared with me he had intended to commit suicide that night and was thankful someone was there to stop and listen to him. Selah! This gives cause for praise! Selah is cause to pause! Selah causes us to reflect! In wisdom, we stop and heed the call to listen.

Reflection

What causes you to pause and to praise God today? What makes you stop and listen to God?

Proverbs 1:2–7

2 For gaining wisdom and instruction;
  for understanding words of insight;
3 for receiving instruction in prudent behavior,
  doing what is right and just and fair;
4 for giving prudence to those who are simple,
  knowledge and discretion to the young—
5 let the wise listen and add to their learning,
  and let the discerning get guidance—
6 for understanding proverbs and parables,
  the sayings and riddles of the wise.

7 The fear of the LORD is the beginning of knowledge,
  but fools despise wisdom and instruction.

Keep on Pushin'

"I have had enough, Lord," he said.
"Take my life; I am no better than my ancestors."
Then he lay down under the bush and fell asleep.

1 KINGS 19:4–5

Sometimes the path you are on takes you in a direction that you had no intention of going. Doors close, but that doesn't mean "I got it wrong." Closed doors, obstacles, or rejection aren't meant to harm you but to *arm* you with knowledge and to boost you toward purposefulness. Sometimes a door shuts just to get you off the couch, out of bed, or out of your head!

Closed doors may not be a *no* but a *not now*. God sometimes uses the path you're on to get you from point A to point B. You're excited, but there may be stumbling blocks or muddy waters to walk through. However, if you keep on pushing with a focus on the Lord, smooth paths and dry grounds await you. This is the time where your trust, your faith, and your character are developed.

It is also the place where the voices of fear and self-doubt speak the loudest. You begin to ask, *Did I really hear God?* Remember Elijah in his confused state after defeating the prophets of Baal? (See 1 Kings 19:1–18 for a vivid biblical example.) In this state of mind, you may want to turn back, question everything, quit, or make everything personal. *I'm being punished for . . . or why didn't I listen . . . or this would never happen if . . . or I'm so stupid . . .*

One evening, I was going to an event that I didn't want to attend, but felt strongly I needed to be there. As I pulled out of my condo's parking lot, it started raining: *Oh, no, my hair*! Halfway down the block, I drove into a torrential storm! I was afraid to pull over because I couldn't see anything in any direction. At that moment, I noticed a car rammed into a tree! All I could think of was turning back or that I had to stop until the rain died down, but I couldn't. I started praying for my safety and the safety of others and proceeded, hoping to be able to see my way clear to pull over. In another fifty feet, I drove onto dry land! Not a drop of water! I felt like I had driven into *The Twilight Zone*. Was Rod Serling going to welcome me? Behind me, it was dark and storming, and ahead clear and smooth driving.

I was glad I pushed through and was not overwhelmed by fear. While in the midst of it, I could not see that the short tempest I went through would soon be over. Unlike God, I can't see down the street, around the corner, up the hill, or into tomorrow. My vision is limited; however, my faith is not, and I knew then, and I know now I can make it.

There will be many times we will run into life's storms, and need to either pull over, stop, or push through inch by inch, taking life one day at a time. We will not always be able to see a solution immediately. This space is where our character develops. This is where we build our faith in God. It is in the storm where you get to meet *yourself*. Bad relationships, failed marriages, job termination, or hard times don't mean you did something wrong. Do not allow yourself to play the *woulda, shoulda, I'm-so-stupid* game! It's an opportunity for you to push.

Push through the unimaginable; push through the mental or physical pain. Push through the FEAR (False Evidence Appearing Real). Push through the mind-fields of others' expectations and *their* rules for *your* life. Beat your own drums! Don't look left or right, just straight ahead, and keep on pushing, because when you PUSH,

Pressures Under Storms Heal!

Reflection

Where are you experiencing a closed door, obstacle, or rejection in your life right now? What do you need from God so that you can push through this period of waiting or struggle? Take time to share your needs with God.

1 Kings 19:11–18

[11] The LORD said, "Go out and stand on the mountain in the presence of the LORD, for the LORD is about to pass by."

Then a great and powerful wind tore the mountains apart and shattered the rocks before the LORD, but the LORD was not in the wind. After the wind there was an earthquake, but the LORD was not in the earthquake. [12] After the earthquake came a fire, but the LORD was not in the fire. And after the fire came a gentle whisper. [13] When Elijah heard it, he pulled his cloak over his face and went out and stood at the mouth of the cave.

Then a voice said to him, "What are you doing here, Elijah?"

[14] He replied, "I have been very zealous for the LORD God Almighty. The Israelites have rejected your covenant, torn down your altars, and put your prophets to death with the sword. I am the only one left, and now they are trying to kill me too."

[15] The LORD said to him, "Go back the way you came, and go to the Desert of Damascus. When you get there, anoint Hazael king over Aram. [16] Also, anoint Jehu son of Nimshi king over Israel, and anoint Elisha son of Shaphat from Abel Meholah to succeed you as prophet. [17] Jehu will put to death any who escape the sword of Hazael, and Elisha will put to death any who escape the sword of Jehu. [18] Yet I reserve seven thousand in Israel—all whose knees have not bowed down to Baal and whose mouths have not kissed him."

Salvation belongs

to the Lᴏʀᴅ:

Your blessing is upon Your people.

Selah

PSALM 3:8 (ɴᴋᴊᴠ)

Positioned for Success

he 1975 movie *Mahogany*, which stars famous African American actors Billy Dee Williams and Diana Ross, gives us a memorable scene. Mahogany (played by Ross) touts her own success by trying to demean her partner, Luther (played by Williams). Luther looks deeply into Mahogany's eyes and says, "Success is nothing without someone you love to share it with."

At Selah, we sisters share our joys, trials, and successes. "When one rejoices, we all rejoice with them" (1 Corinthians 12:26; author's paraphrase), and for the successful Christian woman, it is so meaningful to be able to share our triumphs with sisters.

Success may be defined as the accomplishment of a goal, or some aim, or one's purpose.

From working with so many successful women, including Black, Indigenous, Women of Color, I know society doesn't always lift us up. Many times that trickles down to those close to us in our familiar surroundings. I've had successful bankers share how they didn't even show their awards or plaques to loved ones because of their fear of their partners not being able to handle their success. They felt negative vibes, or even jealousy. Sometimes the jealousy heads toward abuse, in language or other displays, or anger, even rage, because a sister is successful, in the world's eyes. Some in the dominant culture often have a very different definition of a successful Brown or Black woman. It's almost like living two lives: the outward, smile-on-your-face success story the dominant culture sees, and then the "undercover" success story—where you hide the real you until you can get with some "real" people.

One of the words that comes up often on our Selah experiences together is *authenticity*, which is coupled with success. This allows us to really be our authentic *successful* selves, where we celebrate, rather than hate or negate another's accomplishments. One of the reasons I developed the UNSUNG She-Roes awards for multicultural women leaders is because there are so many hidden success stories. If we don't celebrate those who've been elevated by God and our communities and those whom they serve, then who will? Our stories give our lives meaning, and when we are feeling strongly about them, that enhances them.

There are other perspectives: emotional success, successful relationships with family and with others, and one very near and dear to my heart: living the life you want, with purpose, on purpose, and with joy. You *know* when you've arrived, when you've landed smack in the middle of God's perfect will for your life—physically, emotionally, mentally, and spiritually. You know when you've found success in God. Pausing will do that.

If you take the time to be with God, God will take the time to let you know He's been there with you all along. "Lo, I am with you always," Matthew's gospel declares (Matthew 28:20 KJV).

At a certain age and stage, we move from success to significance. The desire to know the meaning of life—the significance of your time here on this earth—becomes central. It's no longer a matter of how many plaques, accolades, and awards one has on her wall. Rather, it's about the relationships that have been built and what you have to show for the time you spent on this planet. There is a day you enter and a day you depart life. However and whenever you take that last breath, significance is the measurement of everything you did or did not do up to and through that last moment.

Was—is—your life one of significance? Have you helped anyone? Have you been a good, moral, ethical soul? Have you blessed anyone? Significance, for many, particularly men, has been measured by job offers, companies merged and acquired, and many external validations. But for women, the nurturers, the caregivers, the givers, how do we live lives of significance? In other words, what do you plan to do with the rest of your life?

Dr. Martin Luther King Jr. had several favorite hymns. One of them was Thomas Dorsey's "Take My Hand, Precious Lord," but that was asking God for something. Another one was, "If I can help somebody, as I travel along, . . . my living shall not be in vain." That is putting the responsibility for action and traction of one's life upon the individual. For me, it may not mean making history books.

Rather, will my children say I was significant as a mother,

a parent, that I mattered? That I tried to make them a priority. Will Christian women leaders say I deposited into and received from them freely, in partnership, as we built God's kingdom? That's significance.

I'd like to think this is the Super Bowl series of our lives, and we are at halftime, and the game is tied. It can go either way. Well, I'm ready to come off the bench and make some winning field goals. Even if I just get one chance to kick that ball, punt, it will be the best kick in the world, and my team-mates and I will be blessed because of the way I played the game. That's significance.

Selah sisters share in our struggles, our joys, and our success. It doesn't just happen during the retreat, but also throughout the rest of our lives. He really is doing a good work in us.

He is a Good Father and Great Shepherd. We can count on God. He is our blessed assurance. He is working all things for the greater good. Let us seek and embrace greater. Stay calm when treading unknown territory. Trust and exercise our faith in Him. His Spirit will guide us. Expect Him to get you there safely. Bless and praise Him for the victory. For what good is success if you don't have someone you love to share it with? Love God, and see what will happen with your life. Then you will be a true success story.

—*Suzan D. Johnson Cook*

The Gift Looks Good

Now Deborah, a prophet, the wife of Lappidoth, was leading
Israel at that time. She held court under the Palm of Deborah
between Ramah and Bethel in the hill country of Ephraim, and the
Israelites went up to her to have their disputes decided.

JUDGES 4:4–5

There is a question that you were born to answer and a
problem you were created to solve. The thought of this
should cause a fire to burn inside you that cannot be
quenched. Deborah was such a woman, who embraced the fire
within her and is known as a great leader of her time. She is an
ideal example of how God chooses and empowers us to carry
out His mission.

I imagine Deborah didn't start life feeling that being Israel's only female judge would be her role. When God appointed
her, though, she stepped into the influential role as judge and
prophetess to lead His people during a time of struggle and
danger. It appears that once she *heard* from God, she didn't let
anyone or anything stop her. She walked in the knowledge that
God chose leaders by *His* standards. She didn't deny or resist
her position in the male-dominated culture and never allowed
gender to hinder her.

Deborah had gifts but, more importantly, she also had a relationship with the *God of her gifts*. Deborah sat in God's presence and listened to Him, and then she prophesied. God can accomplish great things through you when you are willing to listen to and be led by Him. We cannot accomplish God's will using our ways. Deborah was *called*—she realized that her life and her time had been claimed by God. She had heard from Him. She could act because she knew she was chosen by God to be a leader and a wife. She accepted and reflected her ability to do more than one thing well. It doesn't matter who sees you or believes in you as long as you know God called you. This is encouragement to those who feel unseen, unheard, or undervalued. Know today that God called you and His hand is upon you. Deborah was also *consistent*—found rendering judgments for Israel while seated under her palm tree, giving instruction to those in need after stopping to hear from God first. She was highly respected and regarded, because she used her wisdom for all who came to her. She could be counted on to be where she was to be when she was to be there. Deborah was available to God and to others. She used God's wisdom successfully for God. Lastly, Deborah was *confident*; she was full of courage, strength, and character, according to Judges 4 and 5. Her confidence was not in her own ability, but in God's ability to use her. She could be confident, because she knew that all that she accomplished was not in her own power and strength. In Judges 5, we hear her proclaiming the works of the God who created her and continued to use her. After she looked back to see how the Lord brought victory after the battle, she sang a victory hymn. She didn't keep going without stopping to thank

God for what He had done in her life. She paused to give a good God good praise.

God can accomplish great things through us when we are waiting, watching, and willing to be led by Him. God appoints and anoints us for service. The anointing on our life is tied to the needs of others. As we live each day, let us find purpose awakening us and passion fueling us. Someone, somewhere, is counting on what God has placed inside you. Your obedience to listen to God and stand on His words to you makes way for others to fulfill the plan of God in their lives. That's ultimate success.

Judges 4:4–9

⁴ Now Deborah, a prophet, the wife of Lappidoth, was leading Israel at that time. ⁵ She held court under the Palm of Deborah between Ramah and Bethel in the hill country of Ephraim, and the Israelites went up to her to have their disputes decided. ⁶ She sent for Barak son of Abinoam from Kedesh in Naphtali and said to him, "The LORD, the God of Israel, commands you: 'Go, take with you ten thousand men of Naphtali and Zebulun and lead them up to Mount Tabor. ⁷ I will lead Sisera, the commander of Jabin's army, with his chariots and his troops to the Kishon River and give him into your hands.'"

Reflection

What are your gifts? Is anything hindering you from fully operating in them?

How does your relationship with God empower you to use your gifts?

⁸ Barak said to her, "If you go with me, I will go; but if you don't go with me, I won't go."

⁹ "Certainly I will go with you," said Deborah. "But because of the course you are taking, the honor will not be yours, for the LORD will deliver Sisera into the hands of a woman." So Deborah went with Barak to Kedesh.

The Original

**Blessed are those who hunger
and thirst for righteousness,
for they will be satisfied.**

MATTHEW 5:6 (NASB)

*W*hat does it mean to be hungry and thirsty for righteousness? I've had the great fortune of sharing time with sisters, including many prominent women in ministry. They are great examples of living out what it truly means to be hungry and thirsty for righteousness as they serve and advocate for the most vulnerable in society. My connection with these beautiful women inspires me to write about family love and the power of living righteously.

I was blessed with wonderful parents who carried out God's work in the community, at church, and at home. Not until decades after my childhood did I realize that my mother's devoted works deserved the title of *community activism*.

Beyond caring for our family, she dedicated herself to improving the quality of life for senior citizens, the sick, and the shut-in, whenever she could, with me and my brother by her side. She had an insatiable zest for life, allowing nobody to distract her or make her deviate from her paths of righteousness.

Like all of us, she was put on this earth to make a difference in the lives of others, and she did.

Mama was known around town as *The Original Mrs. Meals on Wheels*, long before our township ever developed a formal service. Weekly, she compelled an army of Christian women to join forces, women who donated to and created outreach activities for that cause. They would line up outside the grocery store, armed with grocery baskets and coupons, awaiting her arrival. They each had detailed grocery assignments, gathering items for nothing less than a stellar meal. Often she stood as the only African American woman in the kitchen, and she was never mistaken as anything other than the team leader.

These women would assist her with meal prep in the kitchen, hoping to sneak a peek to repeat her secret recipes in their own homes. They watched over her shoulder as Mother prepared meals from scratch for one hundred to one hundred fifty people weekly, but they couldn't duplicate her scrumptious dishes. She did this with grace, feeling no need to be recognized, or to stand at the podium. She did God's work from behind the counter. She humbly carried out her righteous work assuring that not one person would feel unwelcome, be underfed, or be turned away.

From the eyes of a child, I witnessed through her the care of the "least of these" (Matthew 25:35). Through her, I found out that God provides us with daily opportunities to act with courtesy, love, and kindness. He provides us with the courage to commit and pursue our passions. Now, as a woman and a mother myself, I'm thankful that God shows us daily that our righteous efforts are nonnegotiable. We will face roadblocks and deterrents in our pursuit to live justly. But the strength and courage—along with the hunger and passion—to overcome these obstacles lie within our spirit.

Mama was an example of strength to me; I never saw her compromise her values. She would begin every day with the Serenity Prayer, drink her coffee, and then take on her day. Her standards and her efforts were high yet attainable. She kept her faith, despite experiencing devastating trauma and loss throughout her childhood. My mother never abandoned her curiosities and desires to lead a righteous lifestyle. She was both hungry and thirsty to *make a difference*, leaving a blazing legacy trail behind her. God rest her soul. May we leave a legacy for both the women who share with us at retreat, and all those who will come after us. Thank you, Mama, for teaching me to remain hungry and thirsty for a righteous lifestyle. Thank You, Lord, for lighting and leading the way.

Reflection

What acts of courtesy, fellowship, love, and kindness are part of your legacy?

Matthew 25:31–40

[31] "When the Son of Man comes in his glory, and all the angels with him, he will sit on his glorious throne. [32] All the nations will be gathered before him, and he will separate the people one from another as a shepherd separates the sheep from the goats. [33] He will put the sheep on his right and the goats on his left.

[34] "Then the King will say to those on his right, 'Come, you

who are blessed by my Father; take your inheritance, the kingdom prepared for you since the creation of the world. ³⁵ For I was hungry and you gave me something to eat, I was thirsty and you gave me something to drink, I was a stranger and you invited me in, ³⁶ I needed clothes and you clothed me, I was sick and you looked after me, I was in prison and you came to visit me.'

³⁷ "Then the righteous will answer him, 'Lord, when did we see you hungry and feed you, or thirsty and give you something to drink? ³⁸ When did we see you a stranger and invite you in, or needing clothes and clothe you? ³⁹ When did we see you sick or in prison and go to visit you?'

⁴⁰ "The King will reply, 'Truly I tell you, whatever you did for one of the least of these brothers and sisters of mine, you did for me.' "

The Game Changer

For the Spirit God gave us does not make us timid,
but gives us power, love and self-discipline.

2 TIMOTHY 1:7

*W*e need to take care of ourselves, to ensure our physical and spiritual health is intact. I want to push the envelope to discuss *emotional* health. Each day, we will confront issues of emotional intelligence. The question becomes, What are the consequences if we are spiritually mature yet neglect our emotional life?

I believe the answer to this question is in God's Word.

Throughout the Old and New Testaments, including in the Psalms, we see snapshots of how emotional intelligence played a significant role as to whether or not God's leaders were successful in carrying out their assignments. God expressed a variety of emotions in the Scriptures. God was grieved at the sinfulness of His creation, and the Lord was sorry that He had made humans (Genesis 6:6). Yet His heart was moved by love and compassion toward His people Israel, even when they strayed (Jeremiah 31:20; Hosea 11:8). God even rejoiced over them with singing (Zephaniah 3:17).

From Genesis to Revelation, biblical people express an

array of emotions: anger, joy, sorrow, compassion, forgiveness, and more. The Scriptures reveal that negative emotions can dramatically change a person's life. The Bible shares honestly how an unbalanced emotional life can lead to impulsivity or unhealthy obsessions. We see this in the life of King Saul and his foolish, rash oath after he was rejected as king (1 Samuel 14:24). King David's obsessive relationship toward Bathsheba led to his murder of Uriah, Bathsheba's husband. David arranged for him to be killed in battle (2 Samuel 11:15). These examples demonstrate the destruction and evil that can result from unmanaged emotions.

Emotions are the core of our being, reflecting our attitudes and behavior. The bottom line is that belief alone does not make for a better life; behavior counts. Challenges in our behavior come when any of our emotions control us rather than our controlling them. God never intended for His creation to be ruled by emotions. Therefore, managing emotional intelligence becomes critical for us. The skills needed to display emotional intelligence are self-awareness, self-management, social awareness, and relationship management. These skills help us see the potential in our strengths and weaknesses, which is no small task. Are you up for the challenge?

My understanding of emotional intelligence was severely lacking in my early leadership days. In hindsight, there were moments when I realized I had "blood on my hands" in how I treated and mistreated members of my team. There came a time that I began to understand.

I came to realize that I must courageously step outside of my comfort zone and deal with my emotions. The Bible says,

"Do not conform to the pattern of this world, but be transformed by the renewing of your mind. Then you will be able to test and approve what God's will is—his good, pleasing and perfect will" (Romans 12:2).

In the end, we need to take a deep dive to reflect on how emotional intelligence can be the game changer to bring about transformation in us and in those we are called to serve.

Romans 12:3–18

[3] For by the grace given me I say to every one of you: Do not think of yourself more highly than you ought, but rather think of yourself with sober judgment, in accordance with the faith God has distributed to each of you. [4] For just as each of us has one body with many members, and these members do not all have the same function, [5] so in Christ we, though many, form one body, and each member belongs to all the others. [6] We have different gifts, according to the grace given to each of us. If your gift is prophesying, then prophesy in accordance with your faith; [7] if it is serving, then serve; if it is teaching, then teach; [8] if it is to encourage, then give encouragement; if it is giving, then give generously; if it is to lead, do it diligently; if it is to show mercy, do it cheerfully.

Reflection

Are you giving equal weight to your spiritual and emotional development?
If so, how?
If not, why not?

What will you begin to do today to strengthen your emotional health?

⁹ Love must be sincere. Hate what is evil; cling to what is good. ¹⁰ Be devoted to one another in love. Honor one another above yourselves. ¹¹ Never be lacking in zeal, but keep your spiritual fervor, serving the Lord. ¹² Be joyful in hope, patient in affliction, faithful in prayer. ¹³ Share with the Lord's people who are in need. Practice hospitality.

¹⁴ Bless those who persecute you; bless and do not curse. ¹⁵ Rejoice with those who rejoice; mourn with those who mourn. ¹⁶ Live in harmony with one another. Do not be proud, but be willing to associate with people of low position. Do not be conceited.

¹⁷ Do not repay anyone evil for evil. Be careful to do what is right in the eyes of everyone. ¹⁸ If it is possible, as far as it depends on you, live at peace with everyone.

Flexing with a Purpose

Keep this Book of the Law always on your lips;
meditate on it day and night,
so that you may be careful to do everything written in it.
Then you will be prosperous and successful.

JOSHUA 1:8

When I took time to pause, I realized my definition of success was morphing. Life was coming into clearer focus. Some may call it maturity; others may say this is about life catching up with you. I'd like to say that when I paused long enough to allow God's Word to penetrate me, and for me to hear God, God helped me live the life He created me to live.

My journey to that definition of success began with my returning to the creation account to discover God's purpose in creating me. God created us in the image of God (Genesis 5:1). Scripture clearly states that we were created to glorify God (Isaiah 43:7). Throughout Scripture, God tells us that He has specific plans for us that He has prepared in advance (Jeremiah 29:11; Ephesians 2:10). When I began to journey intentionally to find and fulfill my purpose, I expected to meet obstacles, and to occasionally have doubts. What I didn't expect was to have a moment of crisis when I asked the question, *How bad do I want to understand and fulfill my purpose?*

I understood how to achieve success according to society's definitions and measurements: I had a loving relationship with my husband and children, a corporate career as a vice president with a multimillion-dollar budget, achievement awards, entrepreneurial ventures, lay ministry, and community leadership positions. Yet, there was a pull toward something more. I knew God had placed the desire in my heart, so I followed the pull. And there came a moment that begged the question: *How bad do I want to know and live out God's purpose for me?*

When I was asked to give up what I hold dear, I had to determine how resolute my yes to God was. I asked myself tough questions and in contemplation, I realized my sincerity even as I struggled with my approach. I was set in my ways, but when I let go of the *how*, I found the strength to pursue that which had escaped me: my purpose.

My vision changed, and I realized that all I had experienced was a part of the plan that God had for my life. The good, the bad, the

Reflection

Are you holding on to something that is keeping you from running your race?

• • •

Is your version of success based on what you do, or who you are?

• • •

How can you become more available to live out of your purpose?

best, and the worst all shaped me to do His work. I had to lay some things down, so that I could run the race set before me.

My race is different from the race set before you. When you look over to see me running my race, my twists, turns, and U-turns may look crazy to you. I may look like I'm going in circles. When I arrive at my destinations, you may question, "How in the world did she get there and *why*?" But my success—our success—does not rest in reaching an accolade, position, or destination here on Earth.

I am successful now because I am living the life I was created to live and keeping my eyes on Jesus, aiming for that ultimate destination, where I will be one among the cloud of witnesses (Hebrews 12:1). I press toward the goal of my calling in Christ Jesus (Philippians 3:14). That, truly, is success. I am flexing with that purpose in mind.

Philippians 3:12–14

[12] Not that I have already obtained all this, or have already arrived at my goal, but I press on to take hold of that for which Christ Jesus took hold of me. [13] Brothers and sisters, I do not consider myself yet to have taken hold of it. But one thing I do: Forgetting what is behind and straining toward what is ahead, [14] I press on toward the goal to win the prize for which God has called me heavenward in Christ Jesus.

God Showed Up

Oh, that you would bless me and enlarge my territory!
Let your hand be with me and keep me from harm.

1 CHRONICLES 4:10

first attended the Selah by the Sea retreat in Florida. The resort was beautiful and elegant. The retreat location made me feel like I was royalty. I met former basketball great Julius Erving (Dr. J). Yes, the regular guests were wealthy and famous. The guest speakers at the retreat had experienced success on the world stage. I had the opportunity to sit with a Fortune 500 banker, a big-city news reporter, an ambassador, authors, preachers, and the list goes on. I knew greatness was possible. But what was it that God would have *me* do?

One of the most important lessons I learned while being around these amazing people is that God's blessings are limitless. I had been limiting God's blessings by asking for the specifics I thought up, but God had larger plans. I used to ask God to make me a school principal, but I couldn't even get a job as a vice principal. Throughout my career, I had applied for eighteen different positions as vice principal, and I did not get an interview for one of those positions.

In recent years, I was still asking God for job opportunities based on my limited vision and experience. Just as the country experienced the rise of white nationalist attitudes, I experienced a new supervisor who led our organization in the same manner. My physical, social, and emotional well-being began to deteriorate. I gained weight. I brought my work frustrations home and unfairly directed my anger toward my family. This misery went on for more than a year until one Sunday I felt pains in my chest. The pain was so severe that I asked my husband to take me to the emergency room. I thought I was having a heart attack, but it was an *anxiety* attack. I asked my doctor for medicine to help me sleep. My doctor refused to prescribe medication, instead wisely telling me that I needed to change some things in my life.

I decided that I needed to ask the Lord what He would have me do. Once I got out of my own way, stopped telling God what I wanted, and allowed Him to be God, He showed up and showed out. I feel a hallelujah praise come over me each time I think about His goodness. God led me to run for a seat on the local school board. My election victory propelled me to become the boss of my former supervisor. A year into my four-year elected term as a school board member, God used the West Virginia Twenty-Third Circuit chief judge to elevate me to become a history-making magistrate judge.

God is good and all-powerful. I am so glad that He introduced me to those who could help me expand my vision for what I could become. I began to see that my territory could truly be enlarged beyond my imagination. I learned that what He has done for others, He could do for me. My prayer remains . . .

"God please bless me and increase my territory. Whatever You have for me, please reveal it and allow me to walk in it."

1 Chronicles 4:9–10

[9] Jabez was more honorable than his brothers. His mother had named him Jabez, saying, "I gave birth to him in pain." [10] Jabez cried out to the God of Israel, "Oh, that you would bless me and enlarge my territory! Let your hand be with me, and keep me from harm so that I will be free from pain." And God granted his request.

Reflection

In what areas of your life do you need to pray that God moves and acts on your behalf??

CONCLUSION

I prayed long and hard about how to begin this book, and I prayed even harder about how to conclude, partly because I was so enjoying getting to know the women I've known for years—with even greater depth, love, and joy—through their writings. But also because their stories are so riveting and enjoyable, that I prayed you would enjoy the devotions as much as I.

Sometimes one is biologically born into a family with siblings who are women, and then other times, God allows you to be birthed into an extended family of heaven-sent women, who become family. We share the same DNA, the same Divine Natural Anointing; and the same blood type, the blood of Jesus; and all have the same Father. So I guess we are a "blended" family. The sisterhood that has emerged over these twenty-some years that we have come together and been together on retreats, at conferences, at conventions—even staying connected during the pandemic—has proven to be refreshing, not just for these individual sisters, but also for my soul as host and author.

Sometimes I witness their growth and "aha" revelation moments or breakthroughs as a "proud mama," knowing some of what their journeys entailed. Other times I cry alone or with one of them, splash in the pool with another, or at other times, have gut-busting laughter. Still other times, my spirit and my body are both massaged, both by the Holy Spirit and the anointed hands of our resident masseuse and sister friend. Other stories here remind me of the joy of greeting one another again at retreat after time and tests have passed. So I smiled when I read each of these devotionals.

I guess what I'm saying is that this is not just a book to be read once and put down. It is devotional, filled with unique sets of experiences and worship—and encouragement—filled with the wisdom of those who claim and stand on God's promises and walk in His purpose. I hope *you* will experience over and over again, revisiting, reminding, resetting, repositioning yourself for whatever season, stage of life, and ministry you're in, to be blessed by the Holy Spirit who speaks through the ages and through these pages and sages. Women, sisters—some of us having shared almost four decades together, while others were just born as others of us started our ministries—yet all are wonderful, intergenerational, sensational, and powerful.

Thank you for sharing these parts of our journeys. And I hope it encouraged you not only to read about ours but to have your own selah moments, and to write about and share your own story. We've provided a few pages in our Rest Resources section for you to do so. Let the moments of rest and rejuvenation renew your whole being. Let praise be perched on your lips and published on the pages of your heart. Spread the word that something major happens when God's women selah together, in the Word. . . . And as John wrote, "the Word became flesh" (John 1:14 KJV). We are clear that the Word has dwelt amongst us. For us, Christ was not only absent from an empty tomb; He's been present in the Spirit-filled women, and in the rooms full of Selah by the Sea sisters. Soar, sisters, soar!

—*Suzan D. Johnson Cook*

We are sisters in the eyes of our Creator.

We exemplify God's greatness,
love, and faithfulness.

We remind each other that His love is unwavering.

We illuminate, support, and empower each other.

We are significant, no matter where we live.

We should strive to lead with His knowledge,
His wisdom.

In moments of stillness, in sisterhood, we exalt God.

Let's share a beautiful sunrise or a sunset,
and receive His love and mercy,
and each other's companionship.

Let us be encouraged in our future,
rely on each other's strengths, commit to each other,
with resilience, and compassion.

"For great is his love toward us, and the faithfulness of
the L*ORD* *endures forever. Praise the* L*ORD"* (PSALM 117:2).

—*Maureen "Tarry" Jackson*

Sujay's—Suzan Johnson Cook's—Selah Self-Care Formula

For all women who want to thrive and not simply survive.

- ✓ 24-hour day: 8 hours of sleep (or as many as possible), 8 hours to work, and a few hours to play and "do me" in any form or fashion (do what gives you joy—sewing, reading, lunch with friends, dancing, cooking, etc.)

- ✓ Weekdays: Set times for office hours. Honor them. Have others honor and respect these hours. Use caller ID. Do not feel a need to respond to every text, email, phone call that comes in during your off-hours.

- ✓ Seventh-day rest—Sabbath: Do no business. If you are a clergy or lay leader, then Sunday may not be Sabbath for you. Ministers *work* worship. We are the worship leaders, and CEOs of churches, so it is impossible *not* to work. But be sure to establish a day for your Sabbath, and let everyone have a Memorandum of Understanding (MOU) that you're not available on your Sabbath.

   Because I am also a professional speaker, as well as a preacher, many of my engagements and events are on the weekends. Therefore, I make it my business, my self-care business, to take Mondays as my day to rest and to have Sabbath with God. No alarms. I especially enjoy having the birds—the blue jays and the sparrows—who hang around my window and yard, to sing my wakeup songs. We sing lullabies to put babies to sleep. They sing my "good-morning" songs to awaken me.

✓ Throughout the week:

> Swim 3 to 4 times a week in lap pool for 30 minutes nonstop.

> Treadmill 3 to 4 times a week for 20 to 30 minutes, or walk outside for an hour (3 miles).

> Eat more fruits and veggies. Eat between 12 noon and 7 p.m.

✓ Hire a millennial to handle social media, if you're frequently posting.

✓ Make home a space that brings you joy. I live by the waterside; all my apartments and homes are on or very near the water where I can see amazing sunsets.

✓ Set boundaries: a set time to start and finish the day, or any portion of the day. That includes office hours as well as playtime.

Pause, Pray, and Praise
Pamela Livingston

God wants us to focus on His goodness and faithfulness. He has shared how trustworthy He is in the Bible and through our past victories. He is in control and has all power in His hands. We may not have all of the details as to how things will manifest, but we know He is at work. As you pause in personal retreat, and take some time to be still and listen to God, consider journaling. Write about what God is speaking to your heart.

What is God saying to you? What is He talking about regarding your life? What does Scripture say about this issue or area? And how does this apply to you? And to others? Write a sentence about what the Scripture means to you, and how you will apply it to your life.

Consider these verses—and others you choose—to meditate on and journal about:

- Psalm 5:11: But let all who take refuge in you be glad; let them ever sing for joy. Spread your protection over them, that those who love your name may rejoice in you.

- Psalm 9:2: I will be glad and rejoice in you; I will sing the praises of your name, O Most High.

- Psalm 28:7 (NLT): The LORD is my strength and shield. I trust him with all my heart. He helps me, and my heart is filled with joy. I burst out in songs of thanksgiving.

- Psalm 84:11 (NLT): For the LORD God is our sun and our shield. He gives us grace and glory. The LORD will withhold no good thing from those who do what is right.

- Proverbs 3:5: Trust in the LORD with all your heart and lean not on your own understanding.

- Malachi 3:10: "Test me in this," says the LORD Almighty, "and see if I will not throw open the floodgates of heaven and pour out so much blessing that there will not be room enough to store it."

- John 16:33: I have told you these things, so that in me you may have peace. In this world you will have trouble. But take heart! I have overcome the world.

- Romans 5:3–4: Not only so, but we also glory in our sufferings, because we know that suffering produces perseverance; perseverance, character; and character, hope.

- Romans 8:18: I consider that our present sufferings are not worth comparing with the glory that will be revealed in us.

- Psalm 23:4: Even though I walk through the darkest valley, I will fear no evil, for you are with me; your rod and your staff, they comfort me.

- 2 Corinthians 1:3–5: Praise be to the God and Father of our Lord Jesus Christ, the Father of compassion and the

God of all comfort, who comforts us in all our troubles, so that we can comfort those in any trouble with the comfort we ourselves receive from God. For just as we share abundantly in the sufferings of Christ, so also our comfort abounds through Christ.

- Philippians 1:6 (KJV): Being confident of this very thing, that he which hath begun a good work in you will perform it until the day of Jesus Christ.

- Philippians 4:6: Do not be anxious about anything, but in every situation, by prayer and petition, with thanksgiving, present your requests to God.

- Hebrews 10:35–36: So do not throw away your confidence; it will be richly rewarded. You need to persevere so that when you have done the will of God, you will receive what he has promised.

- 1 Peter 1:8: Though you have not seen him, you love him; and even though you do not see him now, you believe in him and are filled with an inexpressible and glorious joy. ❧

These exciting, authentic, and reflective devotions come from women who understand the meaning of selah because we've experienced it. We're women from all over the world, who come together as wise, sometimes worn-out people, with our calls, our covenants, and our commission from Christ, learning how to make sense out of all of our growth, failures, pain, progress, battle scars, and victories. Just bringing ourselves, our whole selves, broken selves, faith, fears, and dreams. We have the triple Cs as we like to say: we make global connections, have conversations, and enjoy celebrations with one another, and with our God.

Ms. Jetola Anderson-Blair was born in London and grew up in Manchester, Jamaica, and Westchester County, New York. She is a graduate of State University of New York at Plattsburgh and Villanova University. She has been writing for several years and has contributed pieces to *Sister to Sister* devotional (Judson Press) and the *Women of Color Study Bible* (Nia Publishing). *In My Sister's Shoes* is her first solo publication. She was featured in the New York City edition of *Success Guide* as one of "Ten to Watch."

She resides in Houston, Texas, where she and her husband operate a Caribbean restaurant. Her volunteer activities include mentoring high school students, tutoring grade school students, and teaching English as a second language.

Reverend Debora Barr serves as associate pastor of the First Baptist Church of Glenarden, Maryland. She holds a master of divinity and has a passion for teaching, preaching, speaking, and writing about personal intimacy with Jesus, helping to direct people to the unconditional love and healing power of Christ. Debora is the author of *All Things New: A Discipleship Ministry for Life Transformation*, and *Life Transformation Day by Day: A 31-Day Devotional*. DBarrMinistries.org and AllThingsNewLife.org.

Dr. Michelle Boone-Thornton is associate chair and professor of human services at Saint Leo University and the vice president of CMV Communicators, LLC. She completed her doctorate at Regent University in educational psychology and is a registered qualified mental health provider in Virginia. She has authored several journal articles and book chapters, and she presents at colleges, conferences, workshops, and retreats throughout the US and around the world. Dr. Boone-Thornton is a mother of three, has been married thirty-one years, and is a legacy member of Zeta Phi Beta Sorority, Inc.

Reverend Yolanda D. Brown is a minister of economic development, and the visionary founder of Imani's Quest Ministries, a faith-based economic development organization. She is committed to rebuilding: raising up those in desolation, renewing the ruined cities, and doing restorative work. As the spiritual leader of Congregation Destiny, a Sabbath Experience, her emphasis is on helping others *to become* as she seeks to make known the Word of God. Reverend Yolanda lives in New York City and serves the Tri-state area.

Yolanda Caldwell is an entrepreneur, consultant, award-winning facilitator, and international speaker, who is committed to empowering women to live intentionally. She hosts a podcast, *The Heightening*, to equip women to win through faith. A wife and mother, Yolanda is committed to loving her family, succeeding in business, and serving the community. She is currently the director of the Women's Leadership Institute at The College of Saint Rose, Albany, New York.

Pastor Siziwe D. Chili is founder and senior pastor of Hope of Glory Community Church in South Africa. She is also founder and president of Women Arise Fellowship for women infected with HIV/

AIDS or who have suffered abuse, providing them skills development. She is founder and president of Women Arise in Leadership, a support group for women senior pastors. Through Women Arise in Leadership, Pastor Siziwe also mentors, encourages, and gives counsel and guidance to women in a variety of leadership positions.

Beverly Claiborne is the author of *Abiding in God's Word* and CEO of Abide Family Blessings and Amazing Faith Events. She is a speaker with Christian Women in Media Association, and a certified personal life coach. She inspires women to live wisely and live well by applying godly principles. Beverly attended Purdue University. Before stepping out in faith to make Abide products her career focus, Beverly owned a successful interior design firm, and served in management for three nationally known companies. Beverly has been married for more than twenty years to Cary J. Claiborne; they have three children, and one grandson. She resides in Glen Allen, Virginia. abideproducts.com

Teri Coaxum is a mother, grandmother, caregiver, author, motivational speaker, professor, community leader, and owner of Coaxum Connects LLC and Coaxum Connects Wellness Foundation. Under the Obama administration, she served as the U.S. Small Business Administration's Office of Advocacy Regional Advocate for Region II, covering New York, New Jersey, the U.S. Virgin Islands, and Puerto Rico. Prior to her appointment, Coaxum formerly served as the first African American Woman Deputy State Director for Senator Charles Schumer (D–NY) and administrative manager in the Kings County District Attorney's office. Both roles allowed her to advise government officials, advocate for underserved communities, and empower through economic empowerment, job readiness, and technological advancement.

Dr. Caretha Franks Crawford is an award-winning writer, creative designer, blogger, dance minister, pastor, and former associate professor. She is the founder of The Gateway to Wholeness Church

Ministries, In Pursuit of His Presence Worship Arts Ministries, and Caretha Crawford Ministries International in Largo, Maryland. Caretha is the author of five published books and is a graduate of Winston-Salem State University. She holds a master of divinity and doctor of ministry from Maple Springs Baptist Bible College and Seminary. She has one grown daughter, and she lives with her husband in Maryland. She travels extensively, preaching the gospel.

Reverend Tisha Dixon-Williams currently serves as the senior pastor of the First Baptist Church of Bridgehampton in Bridgehampton, New York. As the creator and chief curator of the global ministry movement Who's That Lady?, she conducts in-depth Bible studies that highlight women of the Bible. Her first book, *I See You, Sis: Inspirations from Heroic Women of the Bible Hidden in Plain Sight*, debuted as an Amazon number one bestseller.

Reverend Tish's life is a true reflection of Matthew 6:33: "But seek ye first the kingdom of God, and his righteousness; and all these things shall be added unto you" (KJV).

Gwen Franklin is founder and CEO of B. Lifted Up! Inc., a business and financial consulting company whose mission is empowerment through insight, education, and training. She began her career in radio at Howard University's WHUR-FM, while earning her BA in communications, and she later earned her MBA from Baruch College, CUNY. As a corporate executive, Gwen has implemented campaigns for recording artists that are woven into the fabric of our lives. She served as adjunct marketing professor at New York University and Ramapo College of New Jersey, and is a certificated educator and business administrator in New Jersey. Currently, Gwen attends New York Theological Seminary as a candidate in the master of arts in religious leadership administration program.

Nancy Gavilanes is a speaker, writer, evangelist, and life coach with a heart for encouraging people as they walk by faith and live their God-given dreams. Nancy has authored five Christian living books, has a master's degree in journalism from New York University, and has written for various publications, including the *New York Times* and the *Charisma* website.

Reverend Tamieka Nicole Gerow is a native Philadelphian. She received her bachelor of arts from Eastern University. She enrolled in the master of divinity program as a Kern Scholar at Samuel DeWitt Proctor School of Theology at Virginia Union University, graduating in 2008. While attending STVU, she received a certificate in congregational pastoral care from Virginia Institute of Pastoral Care, Inc. Reverend Gerow is an itinerant preacher, conference speaker, seminar instructor, and retreat facilitator. This proud member of Alpha Kappa Alpha Sorority, Inc., is mother to Kennedy Noelle and Keon Nicholas Xavier. You can follow Reverend Gerow on Instagram @revmrsmom.

Dr. Sheila D. Powell Grimes is a child-centered educational leader and advocate for children and families. She is experienced in improving school-related outcomes in urban education and in coordinating multidisciplinary and multitiered intervention. She strives to ensure equitable access to opportunities for success. She is a skilled professional learning leader and educational consultant. She believes in the power of partnership as a tool to bring about exponential change in the lives of students.

Marcia A. Harris, MD, LHD (HON), graduated from Columbia University Vagelos College of Physicians and Surgeons and trained in internal medicine and gynecology at the prestigious New York Hospital, Weill Cornell Medical Center. She has practiced medicine in New York City for more than thirty years. After suffering a major health crisis about twenty years ago, she changed the focus of her practice to wellness and prevention, utilizing holistic, complementary, integrative, and functional medical modalities.

Maureen Jackson is a chaplain and part of the New York State Chaplain Task Force. She has worked alongside city and state officials in times of crisis and intervention. She has dedicated more than thirty years as an educator in special education and continues to advocate for underprivileged students and their families. Ms. Jackson volunteers as an educator, advocate, and ambassador for the National Alliance for Mental Illness (NAMI), and resides along with her children in New York City and the Greater New York area.

Lieutenant Takana L. Jefferson is command chaplain for Naval Support Activity Washington, DC, and is earning the doctor of ministry degree at Howard University, after completing an MDiv and MBA. Awarded the Captain Stanley J. Beach Leadership award on graduation from Naval Chaplaincy School, Lt. Jefferson has ten years active duty service and eight years in the reserves. She serves as national chaplain for the National Naval Officers Association. Lt. Jefferson served as station chaplain to Headquarters and Headquarters Squadron at MCAS Iwakuni, Japan; as the station chaplain for the United States Coast Guard Academy (CGA) in New London, Connecticut; and as command chaplain on board the USS Emory S. Land in Hagatna, Guam, where she provided counseling services to the Army, Navy, Air Force, Marines, and Coast Guard. Lt. Jefferson served as battalion chaplain, Combat Logistics Battalion 26, Camp Lejeune, North Carolina. She received an impact Navy Achievement medal for her superior care and services of the Marines, and was instrumental in the unit Volunteer Service Award 2018 for Camp Lejeune. Other decorations include Navy and Marine Corps Commendation Medal (3), Coast Guard Commendation Medal, Navy Achievement Medal, Coast Guard Achievement Medal, Navy Good Conduct, Navy Overseas Service, National Defense Service ribbon, and the Joann Miller Community Service award while serving at the Coast Guard Academy. Lt. Jefferson received her Fleet Marines Forces pin while serving 2018 to 2019 at Second Transportation Support Battalion.

Lt. Jefferson is married to Dr. Jonathan K. Jefferson of Cambridge, Massachusetts, and is the mother of one daughter, Jazmyn Scott, of Greensboro, Tennessee, and one son, Antonio Scott, of Albuquerque, New Mexico.

First Lady Trina Jenkins is the devoted wife of Pastor John K. Jenkins Sr. The couple are the proud parents of six children and five grandchildren. In 1976, she accepted Christ as her personal Savior during a service in which her future husband (Pastor Jenkins) was the youth preacher.

Trina Jenkins earned her bachelor of arts in sociology from the University of Maryland, and received an honorary doctor of divinity from Truth Bible College, Jacksonville. As the director of the Family Life Ministries Department at First Baptist Church of Glenarden, Maryland, she oversees more than thirty ministries related to men, women, and families. She also preaches and teaches locally, nationally, and internationally. The Lord continues to use this well-respected, godly woman to train other Christian women to reach their full potential through widely attended First Baptist retreats and conferences that draw women from near and far.

Elizabeth Oroko Kennedy was born in Nigeria and has been in ministry for more than twenty years. She is a mother to John, David, and Charis. Minister Kennedy is studying for her master's in theology, and she is the founder of Women Pray Ministries and publisher of *SHE Magazine*. She is the author of *Wonder Called Woman: How to Enjoy Marital Breakthrough*, and *Turning Your Ideas to Millions*.

Martha Taylor LaCroix—a vibrant and highly positive presence in the singing community—often links her music to civic causes. She has founded the holiday networking organization the Holiday Celebration Club (HCC), the nonprofit for suicide prevention Here's 2 Life, Inc., and Jazzy Fryday, a night of fish dinners and live jazz. Martha received the Los Angeles "Jazz Living Legend Award" in 2016 and was honored as a nominee at the 2018 Billboard Music Awards as a jazz vocalist. She received the "Unsung Shero Award" from Women in the NAACP in 2018. She serves on the advisory board for The Dolo Coker Jazz Scholarship Foundation.

Pamela Livingston is a very grateful born-again and practicing Christian. She is the mother of two adult children. Her business career has spanned more than twenty-five years in corporate and public sectors. God has gifted her with a passion to teach the Bible and to inspire others to trust Him mightily.

Zelrona Mackey is a graduate of The College of the Bahamas with a diploma in Adult Workforce Education and Training, a program she contributed to and designed for cosmetology teachers. She now helps to train all technical vocational teachers in the Commonwealth of The Bahamas. This hardworking woman is a pillar of strength in her home, in her church, in her community, on the Island, and in the world.

Victoria Saunders McAfee is an internationally recognized writer and editor with a passion for POC (People of Color), women's Bible study, and serving others who suffer from sexual abuse issues and emotional pain. Victoria is the author of *Blessed Is She*; *The Sisters' Guide to In-Depth Bible Study*; *Restoring Broken Vessels, Bible Study for Busy Women* and the booklet *Children and Sexual Abuse*. She is a feature writer for *Our Daily Bread* and a curriculum writer for David C. Cook. Victoria earned a bachelor's degree from Ottawa University in counseling psychology. She resides in Milwaukee, Wisconsin, with her husband, David, is mother of three adult children, and grandmother of two.

Jo Anne Meekins is the founder of Inspired 4 U Ministries, LLC, and its imprint Inspired 4 U Publications. She primarily serves as an inspirational author, publisher, and coach. Her mission is to educate, encourage, and empower entrepreneurs to professionalize their online image and increase their visibility, credibility, impact, and income.

Evelyn Miller-Suber is a senior pastor with fourteen years of service in the African Methodist Episcopal Church in New York. She received her master of divinity and doctor of ministry from New York Theological Seminary. She is also a retired human resources professional with a master of public administration from the University of Hartford, Connecticut. Reverend Evelyn considers it a blessed privilege to weave together her pastoral and human resources knowledge for the benefit of ministry.

Reverend Ayanna Kai Mishoe-Brooker, Esq., is happily married to Reverend Johnnie D. Brooker Jr., pastor of Mt. Zion Baptist Church, Dover, New Jersey. Together, they have one son, Johnnie Elisha III, and one daughter, Annaya Kai. Mishoe-Brooker received a juris doctor degree from Seton Hall University and master of divinity with an emphasis in pastoral counseling from Andersonville Theological Seminary. She is the author of *Your Pastor's Wife Needs Your Prayers*, and a contributor to *Soul Sisters: Devotions for and from African American, Latina, and Asian Women*. She is a graduate and lifelong member of Eagle Flight Squadron, Inc., based in East Orange, New Jersey, a nonprofit aviation school for urban youth.

Dr. Barbara L. Peacock is the author of *Soul Care in African American Practice*. She is a spiritual director, teacher, and preacher. She received her master of arts from Princeton Theological Seminary and her doctor of ministry from Gordon-Conwell Theological Seminary. She is married to Gilbert Peacock, and they have one daughter, Vernee.

Reverend Dr. Gloria Miller Perrin is an ordained minister and a certified life coach. She is a graduate of Trinity University in Washington, DC, where she serves as the first protestant chaplain. She holds a master of divinity from Howard University School of Divinity. She earned a doctor of ministry from Regent University in Virginia Beach, Virginia, graduating summa cum laude with a concentration on leadership. Since 2002, she has served as an associate pastor at the First Baptist Church of Glenarden, Maryland. Dr. Perrin recently published her first book entitled *Raising the Bar: Building Authentic Relationships: Transforming Leaders in the Church and Workplace*. Dr. Gloria Miller Perrin is a native of Washington, DC.

Patricia Raybon is an award-winning, bestselling author and journalist who writes top-rated books that help readers move big mountains. A regular contributor at *Our Daily Bread* and DaySpring's (in)courage blog, she is author of several memoirs and devotionals exploring faith, race, and grace. Based in Colorado, Patricia has published *My First White Friend*, her racial forgiveness memoir; *I Told the Mountain to Move: Learning to Pray So Things Change*; and *The One Year God's Great Blessings Devotional*. Her first fiction book, a historical detective romance series featuring "The Praying Detective: The Annalee Spain Mysteries" is scheduled to debut in 2021. Join her on the journey at patriciaraybon.com.

Dr. Marjorie Duncan Reed holds a master of theology and a doctor of ministry from Slidell Baptist Seminary in Louisiana. She is the pastor of St. Paul's Baptist Church in Conshohocken, Pennsylvania, and the first woman to serve as moderator of the 102-year-old Suburban Baptist Association of Southeastern Pennsylvania. She is a hospice chaplain, member of the Baptist Pastors and Ministers Conference, member of the Philadelphia Baptist Clergy Women, and former board member of the Merck Sharp & Dohme Federal Credit Union.

Dr. Elizabeth Rios has been in ministry for more than thirty years serving in various capacities in almost every area of the church, including eleven years as an executive pastor and four as colead pastor. In April 2008, Dr. Liz was asked to serve, and continues to serve, as consulting editor for *Outreach Magazine*, a national magazine for church leaders, pastors, and planters. She was also featured on the cover of the Nov/Dec 2007 issue as a leading Hispanic in America for her work with women and church planting.

Arthena S. Roper has earned three master's degrees: in public administration, teaching, and educational leadership. A philanthropist, she created a foundation that supports students. She is a history-making elected official, appointed by the West Virginia Twenty-Third District Supreme Court Chief Justice to fulfill an unexpired term as County Magistrate. Roper is also an educator, and the creator of social media campaigns named #WeRead_WeLead and Eat~Breathe~Sleep~Vote, emphasizing reading and leadership. Roper writes and designs books that give children of color visuals of success.

Ingrid Vanessa Rushing-Spiva is a wife, mother, and an entrepreneur with an educational background in psychology, child development, and public administration. She is founder and CEO of Community Options Integrated Services, Inc. (COIS), and My Other Office (MOO). COIS agency serves adults with intellectual differences, and MOO is a collaborative creative workspace. As a pioneer in developing California's first Family Home Agency, she recruits providers to host individuals with special needs. Her statewide advocacy and expertise includes state boards and committees.

Pastor Beverly Caesar Sherrod is an anointed and powerful woman of God born in Queens, New York, to the founders of Bethel Gospel Tabernacle. She serves as executive dean for the Bethel Bible Institute, where she is also a faculty member, and is the director of the Bethel counseling ministry. She is a well-known conference speaker, whom God has used to impact the lives of many for His kingdom. She is a graduate of Adelphi University, where she received a master's degree in social work (MSW).

She is married to Pastor John Sherrod and has an adult daughter, Reverend Rhonda Saunders.

The **Reverend Raedorah C. Stewart** serves the body of Christ as a preacher and creative. She is a poet, painter, mother, and public theologian. She is a minister at Covenant Baptist-United Church of Christ (Washington, DC); the faculty director of the Writing Center at Wesley Theological Seminary (Washington, DC); and a committee member in the American Academy of Religion for over two decades. She recently published in *Theology Today* and on the *Evolving Faith Podcast*.

Ms. Venita is an event planner, inspirational speaker, transformative inner peace coach, and the founder/CEO (Chief Empowerment Officer) of The Tyler Marcel Experience. The vision of The Tyler Marcel Experience is to empower women with confidence to (a) master makeup application and not be afraid of using color, and (b) achieve inner healing to create outer beauty using techniques learned through inner peace coaching. The Tyler Marcel Experience offers in-person and virtual workshops to help women reach their greatest potential to create their own signature look and style. At Tyler Marcel, we believe embracing Inner Healing Creates Outer Beauty.

Reverend Dr. Angelique Walker-Smith is senior associate for Pan-African and Orthodox church engagement at Bread for the World in Washington, DC. She brings global, national, and local experience as a faith thought leader, journalist, speaker, and author. Former president Clinton, former senator Richard Lugar, former vice president Mike Pence and two of her alma maters, Yale Divinity School and Kent State University, have awarded her with high distinctions of leadership. She received her doctorate from Princeton Theological Seminary and is the former executive director/minister of the Church Council in Indianapolis, Indiana. She is associated with the National Baptist Convention USA, Inc., is a governance member with the World Council of Churches, and is a president of Historic Black Churches at one of the widest represented ecumenical bodies of Christianity in the United States, Christian Churches Together.

The **Reverend B. Williams Waters** represents the fourth generation of ordained ministry in her family as an itinerant elder in the African Methodist Episcopal Church. She serves on the executive staff at Abundant Life A.M.E. Church, Dallas, Texas, where the Rev. Dr. Michael W. Waters is founding pastor. She heads the publications ministry providing weekly updates to members and ministry partners.

Waters earned her BFA in interior design at Texas Tech University, Lubbock, Texas, and her MFA at Southern Methodist University, Dallas, Texas. She also studied at the Houston Graduate School of Theology.

She is a published author, a playwright, and a prolific songwriter. Her devotion, "A Cloud of Witnesses," is included in the book, *Our Help: Devotions on Struggle, Victory, Legacy*, published by Our Daily Bread Ministries. Several of her plays were produced in local venues and her songs were recorded on albums.

Trudell Webster is married to Rev. Dr. Dwight Webster, the founder and pastor emeritus of Christian Unity Baptist Church, New Orleans, who is also the senior pastor of Beth Eden Baptist Church, Oakland, California. They are parents to four sons. She is a professional licensed massage therapist, massage educator, and lecturer. The Webster family experienced displacement to California during Hurricane Katrina, and continue to thrive in ministry on the West Coast while retaining ministry roots in New Orleans.

Dr. Judy Williams is an executive management professional and business owner with more than twenty years of experience in IT preparedness and strategic and business planning. Keenly focused on strategic planning, management, and brand development, she is passionate about assisting clients in the areas of operational readiness and execution, including vision realization. Her nonprofit involvement and board affiliations include being senior advisor to People for People, Inc.; Zion Theological Seminary; On Our Own of Montgomery County; and City Bible College. Dr. Williams is excited about the possibilities unfolding in her personal and professional life, as she gains further clarity of her purpose within the for-profit and non-profit, small to large corporate and business arenas, as well as developing and marketing family-owned land.

Thelma K. Williams is a seasoned public health professional with a passion for adolescent and international health. She received her bachelor of science in public health administration from Rutgers University; and her master's degree in public health in Community Health Education from Hunter College. A native of New York, she currently resides in Atlanta, Georgia. An active golden lifetime member of Delta Sigma Theta Sorority Inc., she began her career at local and state government, and community-based organizations in New York, and then served at the federal and now international level. Her life purpose is to mentor and empower young people to be their authentic self. She is a member of the Gwinnett Citizens Academy, a founding member of the Global Black Women's Chamber of Commerce, and a volunteer for Moving in the Spirit.

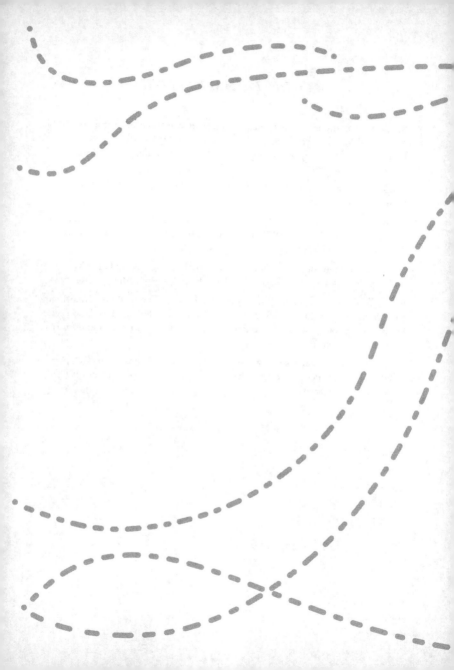

Other Books by
Suzan D. Johnson Cook

Sister to Sister: Devotions for and from African American Women
(Judson Press), 1995

Too Blessed to Be Stressed: Words of Wisdom for Women on the Move
(Thomas Nelson), 1998

Becoming a Woman of Destiny: Turning Life's Trials into Triumphs
(TarcherPerigee), 2010

Soul Sisters: Devotions for and from
African American, Latina, and Asian Women
(TarcherPerigee), 2016

The Sister's Guide to Survive and Thrive in Ministry
(Judson Press), 2019